D1509356

Bullmastiffs

Ch. Graecia Centaur and his daughter, Helga of Graecia.

BULLMASTIFFS
AN OWNER'S COMPANION

Alan and Mave Rostron

Distributed by
Trafalgar Square
North Pomfret, Vermont 05053

The Crowood Press

First published in 1999 by
The Crowood Press Ltd
Ramsbury, Marlborough
Wiltshire SN8 2HR

British Library Cataloguing-in-Publication Data

A catalogue record for this book is available from the British Library.

ISBN 1 86126 202 7

Dedication
To all the dogs we have owned, without whom this book would not have been
possible.

Acknowledgements
The authors would like to thank the many people who contributed and helped with
the writing of this book: Mr Graham Wood, for his help and advice, along with the
time he spent at the computer; Hazel, for her invaluable proof-reading; Mr Phillip
Robinson of The Kennel Club library staff for his diligence and research assistance;
Mrs Kerry Cannon of Australia for supplying information on showing and judging
in Australia; and Mr Andrew Burt of Australia, Mr and Mrs Keith and Gail Warren
of New Zealand, Mrs Nadia Coen and Mr Ted Earys of Southern Africa, and Mr and
Mrs Alfred Adaikalaraj of Malaysia, who all supplied information and/or
photographs from their respective countries.
    Finally, we would like to acknowledge the help given by The Kennel Club, The
American Kennel Club, The Australian National Kennel Council, The Canadian
Kennel Club, The Finnish Kennel Club, The Netherlands Kennel Club, The New
Zealand Kennel Club, and The Kennel Union of Southern Africa.

Picture Credits
Animal Pics, page 195; C. M. Cooke, pages 12, 26, 30, 131; David Dalton, pages 29, 83,
112, 144; Derby Evening Telegraph, page 17; Frank Garwood, page 199; Norman
Greville, page 20; John Hartley, page 172; Russell Fine Art, frontispiece.

Line-drawings by M. Rostron

Edited and designed by OutHouse Publishing Services

Printed and bound in Great Britain by WBC Book Manufacturers Ltd,
Mid Glamorgan

Contents

1

History of the Breed

Origins

It is not our intention to go too deeply into the origins of the Bullmastiff. Obviously, the breed's history prior to the first officially recorded Kennel Club entries can only be researched from other sources, not all of which can be relied upon. In any case, as this subject has already been extensively and satisfactorily covered by other authors (*see* Bibliography) we would like to offer only a brief theory as to the possible origins of the Bullmastiff prior to the start of the twentieth century.

To discover the early dogs from which our Bullmastiffs evolved, it is necessary to travel back to pre-Roman times, when there is evidence that invaders were met by fighting dogs of massive size. Traders with Britain possibly brought these animals with them, and the descendants of the dogs were trained by their owners to help them in battle. That these dogs were both efficient and terrifying has been verified in Roman reports applauding their courage and ferocity in battle, and their numerous appearances in various Roman art forms and Greek and Egyptian friezes also suggest that they were held in high esteem.

These dogs were first mentioned by the Roman Gracius Faliscus, who referred to them as Pugnaces, while Claudian called them the 'broadmouthed dogs of Britain'. Many were sent to Rome by the Procurator Pugnacium, an official appointed by Rome whose job it was to ensure a continual supply of these dogs for the amphitheatres of Rome. There they were pitted against gladiators, lions, tigers, bears, and other huge dogs.

In his *Anecdotes of Dogs* (1858), George R. Jesse described these fighting dogs as 'A dog of gigantic size, of a yellowish colour, with a black muzzle'. This description seems to tally with that of mollossors, large mastiffs from the Mollossi region of ancient Greece which were used extensively for their performance in the arena, and from which some experts believe all mastiff types are descended. Remains of mollossors have been found in Britain, together with dogs of a smaller type and conformation, but were the mollossors ancestors of the dogs taken from Britain for use in Roman arenas or were these dogs native to Britain?

By the time of the Roman invasion of Britain the mollossor type of dog had spread over most of Europe and Asia. Therefore logic tells us that there must have been some factor which made the dogs from Britain sufficiently desirable to the Romans to export them to Rome, even though there must have been numerous sources of mollossor-type dogs closer to hand. We believe that the mastiff type of dog that arrived in Britain originally was subsequently crossed with native British dogs to produce something superior to the mollossor. As mentioned above, remains of smaller mastiffs have been found together with the larger specimens, and it is possible that these smaller types could have been the forebears of the smaller mastiffs that were used for guarding, and later used in bear-baiting and bull-baiting (*see* below). So, while many researchers suggest that mastiff-type dogs originated from the mollossors, we believe instead that other large dogs of native origin could have been bred with a European type of mastiff, possibly a diminutive from the mollossors, but not necessarily so.

While an apparent difference in mastiff size existed for many centuries it was not taken into general consideration until comparatively recently, when writers described mastiff types of two sizes: one big and ponderous; the other a dog which, although powerful and solid, was smaller in stature and was used for guarding and other domestic purposes. The fact that these smaller dogs spent much of their lives chained up may have earned them their name of bond-dogs or bandogges. It would appear that the small mastiffs could possibly be a predecessor of our modern Bulldog, which, if true, indicates a close kinship between the breeds. In his book *The Staffordshire Bull Terrier*, J. F. Gordon writes, 'In the 15th century we are introduced to the Alaunt or Alan, names which appear in *The Master of Game* written by Edward, Second Duke of York, between 1406 and 1413: "A dog of large bull-dogge proportions it is described as short headed, pugnacious and inclined to hang on to anything attacked"'.

The first serious attempts to classify dogs and make a proper division of the breeds according to their functions, appearance, and names occurred in 1570. This classification took the form of the

De Canibus Britannicus, by Dr Johannes Caius (who was the founder of Caius College, Cambridge, and physician to Queen Elizabeth I). It was written in Latin and later translated into English by Abraham Fleming in *Of English Dogges* (*see* Bibliography). Here the mastiff or bandogge is described as 'An huge dogge, stubborne, eager, burthenous of body, and therefore of but little swiftness, terrible and fearful to behold, and more fearse and fell than any arcadian curr'. At that time all large dogs would have been termed a mastiff, but in his description Caius suggests there were at least two sizes of mastiff: a large, heavily built dog and a smaller, more agile type of dog used for guarding and fighting.

A further differentiation between the large and small mastiff types occurred with the implementation of forestry laws decreeing that mastiffs and all dogs of a similar size that would not fit through a standard gauge should be 'expeditated'. The practice of expeditating was most barbaric and cruel, and was intended to make it impossible for a dog to hunt the king's game. The procedure was carried out by the King's Regarder, in which three of the animal's toes were removed. The description of how this was done appeared in *A Treatist of the Lawes of the Forest* (1615) by John Manwood and is reproduced in Clifford Hubbard's *The Bullmastiff*: 'The mastiff brought to set one of his forefeet upon a peece of wood of 8 inches thicke, and a foot square, the one with a mallet setting a chisel of 2 inches broad upon the three clawes of his forefoot at one blow doth smite them clean off'. We believe that this practice tended to make people favour the more diminutive type of mastiff, which would be small enough to avoid mutilation but which would still make a capable guard dog.

In the eighteenth century authors began to differentiate further between the mastiff types. In editions of *Histoire Naturelle*, for example, Buffon wrote, 'The bull dog with the mastiff produces a mongrel which is called the strong bull dog and is much larger than the real one, and approaches it more than the mastiff'. References were also made to a similar type of dog in *The Sportsman's Repositary* (1820) by John Lawrence as 'smaller mongrels and mastiffs', and later to a mastiff which 'might have had a dip or two of the Bull Dog blood in him'. Throughout the nineteenth century there were further mentions of mastiff-bulldogs, bull-mastiffs, and gamekeepers' night dogs.

Many people appear to be under the impression that the Bullmastiff is a modern production, but as Arthur Craven, author of the first book dedicated solely to Bullmastiffs (*see* Bibliography), states:

The Bullmastiff has been with us for hundreds of years, and what is more, in its early career it was just as pure in breeding as it is today. As far as I can ascertain, the only difference between the old and the modern type as far as purity of breeding goes it is that whilst our forefathers bred animals with a 50/50 blood mixture, we today breed stock on the 60/40 basis in order to produce a type of dog that is more suitable for our present requirements.

Arthur Craven was a championship show judge of Bullmastiffs, and as an author researched his subjects in great depth. An advertisement reprinted in his book, *The Bullmastiff As I Know It* (*see* Bibliography), makes the point that there was a definite type of Bullmastiff over two hundred years ago. His coverage of the history of the breed also dealt with bull-baiting, a very popular sport for over 600 years in which good dogs were highly prized. The dogs used for bull-baiting were developed over the centuries to become smaller, more muscular, and more agile, with a head and muzzle more suited to pinning down a bull. Craven makes comment on the bull-baiting events that took place in 1795 at Chorlton-cum-Hardy, Manchester, at which bull and mastiff dogs owned by one Thomas Smith, a butcher in Manchester, were used for bull-baiting on more than one occasion. Today the bullring is Chorlton Green, which stands between St Clement's Church and the Horse & Jockey Inn. At least two hostlers in Chorlton at that period hired out bulls for baiting, and the events aroused tremendous interest, with hundreds of spectators journeying from Manchester to Chorlton (at that time a small village) to witness what they probably termed a good afternoon's sport.

It is our opinion that a bull and mastiff type of dog has been in existence for many centuries. When at a later date these were crossed with the English mastiffs two distinct types were brought together, which in theory emanated from the same origins.

Early Twentieth Century

The first two years of the twentieth century saw a Mr Burton taking an active part in demonstrating the capabilities of the keeper's night dog, in particular with his own dog Thorneywood Terror. The format was to securely muzzle the dog and then release him to chase after a man who had been given a good head start. The dog would soon overtake his 'victim' and bring him down, whereupon he would then pin the man to the ground and hold him secure until he was removed. As far as we are aware, nobody ever bettered the dog.

A report in the *Daily Express* on 1 August 1900 reads as follows:

The First Annual Gamekeepers Dog Show at the Aquarium, August 1st 1900. Among the dogs there were the Bull-Mastiff, an especially interesting and versatile dog. He can see in the dark and hear like an ear trumpet. In peace he can be used for pinning poachers and trespassers; in war he would be as good as ten sentries, he looks like a cross between a Bulldog and a Demon. Unlike the Bulldog, who is a gentleman at peace with all the world until he has cause for war, the Bull-Mastiff has a perpetual grievance against society and has a cheerful habit of pulling it down on sight. Hence his usefulness as a Watch Dog. Yesterday he gave striking illustrations of his strength and fierceness. Although muzzled, he pulled down strong men as if they were empty suits of clothes, and worried them so realistically that ladies screamed.

The Field reported of the 1901 Show:

Mr Burton of Thorneywood Kennels brought to the show a Night Dog and offered any person one pound, who could escape from it while securely muzzled. One of the spectators who had had experience with dogs volunteered and amused a large assembly of sportsmen and keepers who had gathered there. The man was given a long start and the muzzled dog slipped after him. The animal caught him immediately and knocked down his man with the first spring. The latter bravely tried to hold his own, but was floored every time he got on his feet, ultimately being kept on the ground until the owner of the dog released him. The man had three rounds with the powerful canine but was beaten each time and was unable to escape.

The dog in question weighed only 90lb (40kg), thus proving the point that a dog in fit, muscular condition has no problems in fulfilling his role. Such a dog is definitely far better than some of the overweight, out-of-condition animals we see today.

The Bullmastiff proceeded to develop under such stalwarts as Mr Burton, without whose help and foresight the breed would have had a much harder time in becoming established. These people included Mr J. Biggs of the Osmaston Kennels; Mr J. H. Barrowcliffe, who later became the first president of the Midland Bullmastiff Club; Mr J. Barnard, a very well-respected figure; Mr S. E. Mosley of Farcroft Kennels; and Mr V. Smith of Pridzor Kennels.

Mr Mosley of the Farcroft Kennels was a force to be reckoned with in the early years, and to the thinking of the majority of people associated with the breed today he was the person responsible for creating the modern Bullmastiff. Although this is probably true, it must be remembered that not only those named above but also many others were just as dedicated, and that we owe them all a debt of gratitude.

In his booklet Mosley sets out his method for producing his type of dogs as follows:

> Taking a mastiff bitch and a bull-dog I produce 50/50, a bitch of that I mate to a mastiff dog, and this gave me a 75% mastiff and a 25% bull-dog bitch, which I mate to a 50/50 dog. A bitch from this litter, 62.5% mastiff and 37.5% bull-dog, I mate to a 50/50 dog, and a bitch from this litter I put to a 62.5% mastiff and a 37.5% bull-dog. Which gave me approximately my ideal 60% mastiff and 40% bull-dog.
>
> I repeat this from other bloodlines as an outcross, thus I establish my Farcroft strain, and the Bull-Mastiffs standard breed of type set, which breeds true, like produces like.

Mosley's motto read 'Farcrofts are what Bull-Mastiffs should be. Faithful and fearless, but not ferocious. Big enough to be powerful, but not too big to be active'. It is safe to say that Mosley commented on several occasions, in fact boasted about the fact, that he only used

Mr Vic Smith of Pridzor Kennels judging Ch. Bulstaff Achilles (left, with Mr Ralph Short) and Ch. Dancer of Oldwell (with Mr Harry Colliass).

in his crossings mastiff and bull-dogs, and at no stage did he use any other breeds. (May we reiterate at this stage that the bull-dogs used were in no way similar in size or conformation to present-day Bulldogs. They were probably, we believe, directly descended from true working stock.) Mosley was rewarded for his early efforts by having the honour of breeding the first ever champion, Ch. Farcroft Silvo, a bitch. His dog Farcroft Fidelity was the first Bullmastiff to win a first prize in an approved class scheduled for Bullmastiffs, held at Bagnall in 1925.

While Mr Mosley claimed that this was exactly how he came about his method, we have found through our experience of crossing breeds to produce working Lurchers that it is not as straightforward as his formula suggests. There are pitfalls to this kind of breeding, and it must be appreciated that a large number of animals produced by these methods are quite unsuitable for use in future breeding programmes. Indeed, the fixing of type in this way is fraught with very many disappointments along the road to fruition. Unfortunately, breeders in the past attempted crosses of various kinds in an effort to correct parts of the dog as they thought fit. This may or may not have had the desired effect, but as we do not know the conditions of stock available at that time nor the corrections they were striving for, we feel we cannot devalue these crossings as so many others have done. We should also always bear in mind that many other breeds have been much improved by introducing genes from another source and then breeding back to the original stock.

The Bullmastiff pure-bred was officially recognized by The Kennel Club in December 1924. *The Kennel Club Gazette* (number 537) entry reads as follows:

> With reference to the Bull-Mastiff, the committee, at their meeting of the 2nd inst., decided that it is prepared to open a section among the 'Any Other Variety' registrations for Bull-Mastiffs, if pure-bred as such, and when sufficient be registered under this heading according to the scale mentioned above, the breed would be eligible for a place in the Register of Breeds. It is, of course, most important to observe the distinction between a Bull-Mastiff pure-bred and a Bull-Mastiff cross-bred, the former being a dog bred with both parents and the preceding three generations, without the introduction of a Mastiff or a Bull-Dog. The term Bull-Mastiff cross-bred implies the existence of a definite cross, which has not yet been bred out according to regulation 12, of the Regulation for Registration.

13

In 1925 the Midland Bull and Mastiff Club was informed by The Kennel Club that they, The Kennel Club, could not accept the Midland club's proposed Standard of Points for the Bullmastiff, as it was not their policy to publish a standard of points for any breed. In 1926 the National Bull-Mastiff Police Dog Club was officially recognized, and very soon afterwards The Kennel Club accepted a Standard for the Bullmastiff, which had been produced by Mr Mosley. The two standards being applied at that time were very similar, the main differences being a 1in (2.5cm) variation in the height limit and a ½in (1.2cm) variation in the length of the muzzle. Until the parties concerned later agreed on a Standard, we believe that this was the only period in the history of the breed when two standards were in use at the same time. It must have been very confusing for the judges!

At Crufts in 1926 the breed had one class, of course, with no Challenge Certificates on offer. It was judged by Mr S. Graham, who found his winner in Mr Mosley's Farcroft Fidelity; second was Morris's Stand By, and third place went to Aldred's Topsy's Brutus. The following year there were eight classes scheduled for the breed, to be judged by Mr J. W. Marples. There was an increase in the total entry to forty-seven dogs. Mr Marples' main winners were Farcroft Fidelity and Farcroft Silvo.

In October 1927 The Kennel Club agreed that the Bullmastiff pure-bred should be added to the Non-Sporting Section of the Register of Breeds.

The 1928 Crufts Show saw Bullmastiff Challenge Certificates on offer for the first time. The dogs who made history on the day, under Judge H. R. Brown Jr, were Mr V. J. Smith's Tiger Prince, winner of the dog Challenge Certificate, and Mr S. E. Mosley's Farcroft Silvo, winner of the bitch Challenge Certificate. Second in the Open dog class was Athos and third was Farcroft Finality; in the Open bitch class Farcroft Trailer was second and Noble was third. Farcroft Silvo went on to become the breed's first champion, gaining her title in three consecutive shows: Crufts, Manchester (judged by S. Graham), and The Kennel Club Show (judged by R. S. Whitson). Later, Tiger Prince became the first male champion. The fourth set of Challenge Certificates on offer that first year was at Birmingham. The judge on the day was Count V. P. Hollender, who found his dog Challenge Certificate winner in Farcroft Fidelity and bitch Challenge Certificate winner in Ch. Farcroft Silvo, both of which were owned by Mr Mosley.

In November 1929 Mr Toney's Ch. Roger of the Fenns was born, bred by Mr G. F. Wedgewood. This is probably one of the dogs that have had the most influence on modern-day Bullmastiffs, and we suspect that there are very few dogs today whose pedigree cannot be traced back to him in some way. Most kennels of the earlier breeders were based on Ch. Roger of the Fenns as he was much used as a stud at the time. Mr Toney also owned Ch. Peter of the Fenns and Ch. Torfrida of the Fenns.

While it is not possible in this book to include every single person or kennel involved with Bullmastiffs, we would like to mention those who in our opinion were instrumental in the early days of the breed, trying to fix type and at the same time increase the general public's awareness of the Bullmastiff. They struggled under difficult times and conditions, especially through World War II and the years immediately after. Food for the dogs was not easy to obtain in sufficient quantities, and long-distance travel was still a daunting proposition, if possible at all – the idea of travelling across the country for a mating would have been out of the question, except in very exceptional circumstances. Most breeders of today would have no concept of the trials and tribulations these early breeders had to contend with; they were indeed determined people.

Mrs Murray-Smith was one such breeder, who owned Athos, Ch. Wisdom of Wynyard, and Ch. Jeanie of Wynyard. Wisdom was bred by the Marquis of Londonderry and Jeannie was bred by Mrs Murray-Smith herself. Mr Jim Higginson of the Stanfell Kennels must be remembered for Ch. Boy of Stanfell, Ch. Duchess of Stanfell (owned by a past chairman of the Bullmastiff Association, Mr Bill Burgess), Ch. Beppo of Bulmas, Ch. Beppo of Stanfell, Ch. Beauty, Ch. Major of Stanfell, Ch. Billy of Stanfell, Bambi of Stanfell, and many more.

Mr Larry Spruce, who lived in Sale on the outskirts of Manchester, must be remembered for his two very famous prefixes, Brooklands and Rodenhurst. His dogs included Ch. Roger of Brooklands, Ch. Jeanette of Brooklands (bred by T. Pennington), Ch. Rodenhurst Masterpiece, and Ch. Rodenhurst Marksman. Ch. Rodenhurst Masterpiece and his son, Ch. Rodenhurst Marksman, were dogs of undoubtable quality and had a great influence in the Northwest; in particular, they played an important role in the foundation of the Misses Goodhall's Goodstock Kennels.

Mr and Mrs Morris of the Gwydyr Bullmastiffs also lived in Sale close to Mr Spruce and must be remembered for their fine dog Ch. St

David of Gwydyr, sired by Ch. Loki of Mullorna. Another near neighbour of Mr Spruce was Mr Tom Pennington, who lived a couple of miles away in Stretford, and who was the proud owner of Ch. Bubbles. Mr A. Pennington owned Ch. Arpens Peter Pan. This small area of Sale, Stretford, Stockport, and Chorlton-cum-Hardy, approximately 10sq miles (25sq km) in total, has always had a strong Bullmastiff contingent, most of whom we met and talked to when we first became involved with the breed.

Miss J. Lane owned Ch. Castlehill Peggy Ann and Ch. Athos. Athos had previously belonged to and been campaigned by Mrs Murray-Smith. The renowned Mrs D. Mullins of the Mullorna prefix also appeared on the scene in the 1930s, and was making a great name for herself with Ch. Loki of Mullorna, Ch. Buddy of Hickathrift, Ch.Tenz, and Rodian. Mullorna was well known for the deep, rich, deer-red colour so rare in the breed today. It is believed that Rodian would also have become a champion had it not been for the war.

Mrs G. E. Hill and her partner, Mr Cyril Leeke of the world-renowned Bulmas Bullmastiffs, began breeding in the late 1920s. The first Bulmas litter to be registered at The Kennel Club was out of a bitch, Sheila of Bulmas, bred by Mr S. Pattisch. Some other famous Bulmas dogs include Ch. Wendy of Bulmas (their first champion), followed by Ch. Billy of Bulmas, Ch. Beppo of Bulmas, Ch. Branch of Bulmas, Ch. Bulldozer, Ch. Billagain of Bulmas, Ch. Battle Royal of Bulmas, and Ch. Beppoagain of Bulmas, to name but a few. In our opinion the Bulmas Kennel made the biggest impact on the breed of any kennel or group of breeders dating right from the early 1900s, including Mr Mosley, until the emergence of the smaller, more compact kennels of the 1960s and 1970s (in particular Buttonoak, Goodstock, Bulstaff, and Oldwell).

Others involved in the development of the breed include Mr Massie, also associated with the Barton area of Stretford, who bred Ch. Bartonville Red Sultan, and Mr Tom East, a well-known enthusiast with Ch. Grantirk Grundy. Mrs Dorothy Nash campaigned her well-known red dog Ch. Robin Hood of Le-Tasyl, while Mr E. Burton of the Navigation Kennels (not to be confused with Mr Burton of Thorneywood Kennels) bred Ch. Navigation Terror. Mr Tom Avery bred the really outstanding dog Ch. Magician of Bablock and also owned Ch. Billy of Stanfell, who, along with the all-time great Ch. Roger of the Fenns (bred by Mr G. F. Wedgewood), was the only dog during this period to sire ten champions. Mr and Mrs Ted Warren of

Mr Tom East with Ch. Granturk Grundy and Ch. Granturk Griffin.
(1950.)

Harbex fame bred the unforgettable dog Ch. Chips of Harbex, who later became the first brindle male champion for a great many years. Without the dedication of the Warrens to dogs of the brindle colour it is certain that not only would there have been far fewer today, but that they would have been of a much lower quality.

Major Clifford Derwent used the Paris-Garden prefix, and must have put a great deal of thought into its selection (Paris Gardens, in London, was the site of the Elizabethan bear and bull pits). Major Derwent's most memorable dog was Ch. Major of Stanfell. He spent a great deal of time in his early days trying to perfect the breeding of what he called the Regency Bulldog, which would have been a very impressive type of dog.

Last but not least, we cannot close this section without mentioning the indomitable Mr Vic Smith of the Pridzor Kennels. As mentioned earlier, Mr Smith had the honour of owning the first ever British Bullmastiff dog champion, Ch. Pridzor Tiger Prince. Other Pridzor dogs that contributed to modern-day Bullmastiffs were Ch. Pridzors Ideal, Ch. Pridzors Reward, and Ch. Pridzors Trust.

In 1931 the British Bullmastiff League was formed from the defunct Midland Bull and Mastiff Club. In October 1933 the breed was formally recognized by The American Kennel Club. The Bullmastiff Association was formed in 1934 to accommodate the ever-increasing following of Bullmastiff fanciers in the Northwest, while in 1935 the Southern Bullmastiff Society and Training Club was formed to cater to the large number of Bullmastiffs in the London area. The Standard was revised by the Southern Bullmastiff Society and Training Club in 1943, when it took on a different format to previous standards. Just after World War II, in 1946, the Welsh Bullmastiff Society was formed (in 1961 its name changed to the Welsh and West of England Bullmastiff Society).

Late Twentieth Century

Continuing on the solid foundations laid down by the early breeders and enthusiasts, the breed has continued in the hands of some very capable and far-sighted activists. Again, due to lack of space we cannot mention them all but have presented those who in our opinion have contributed most to the breed in the last fifty years.

The 1940s

We must begin this section with the Wyaston Bullmastiff Kennels, founded by Mr Douglas B. Oliff, who as far as we know has been involved with Bullmastiffs 'for ever'. We became associated with Bullmastiffs in 1958, and at that time Mr Oliff was already a long-established breeder. The most memorable dog he bred was Ch. Wyaston Tudor Prince, owned by Dr J. Clarke. He was out of Wyaston Tudor Lass and sired by Wyaston Captain Cuttle, who will always be remembered as the dog who was photographed wearing the antique spiked war dog collar.

Mr Gerald Warren of the Copperfield prefix has been around since the mid-1940s, and in 1972 made up Ch. Copperfield Martin Chuzzlewit, followed in 1973 by Ch. Copperfield Sarah Pocket, a really outstanding bitch. Mr Warren also bred Ch. Copperfield Ben

Beryl Colliass with Ace at Oldwell House.

Allan, owned and shown by Mr and Mrs A. Wood, Ch. Copperfield Sam Weller, and the good-sized bitch Ch. Copperfield Maria Lobbs. In 1984 he made up Ch. Copperfield Pip. After illness Gerald, although still in command, found it difficult to handle the dogs at shows and his son Billy took over the responsibilities. He campaigned to his title Ch. Copperfield Captain Bailey at Crufts in 1995. In 1997 the Copperfield prefix was officially transferred to Mr Billy Warren.

In 1949 Mr and Mrs Terry began their famous Buttonoak Kennels, and showed such outstanding dogs as Ch. Swatchway Amethyst of Buttonoak, Ch. Ambassador of Buttonoak, and Ch. Ambassadorson of Buttonoak, who went on to win Reserve Best in Show at Crufts in 1958. Ch. Alard of Buttonoak, Ch. Anthony of Buttonoak, and Ch. Bimbi of Buttonoak were exceptional dogs for the time, and apart from Ch. Anthony of Buttonoak were slightly lighter in build than the average Bullmastiff of the day while at the same time being well-balanced and of a good overall quality.

The late 1940s saw the rise of Mrs Millard and Mrs Eaton of the famous Marbette Kennels. This was the first registration of the Marbette prefix, although it has since been re-registered in the name of Armstrong-Carter. The Marbette Kennels bred some really out-standing dogs, and in particular they had success with Master of Marbette, who later gained his title and went on to produce well-known dogs such as Ch. Mi-Brandy of Marbette, Ch. Master Brandy of Marbette, Ch. Mi-Hope of Marbette, and Ch. Mi-Choice of

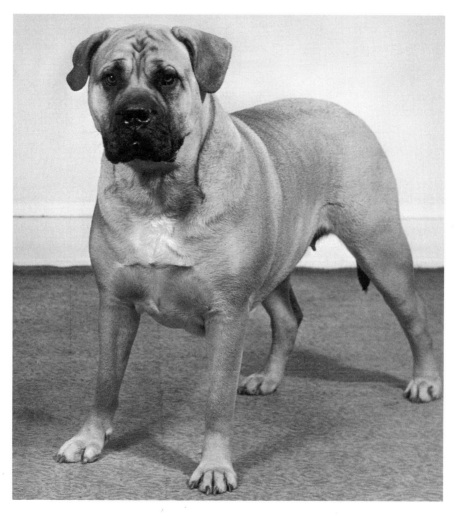

Ch. Bambino, the first Oldwell champion.

Marbette. Another very good dog was Mr H. Colliass's Ch. Oldwell Mi-Trooper of Marbette. The Marbette Kennels was well known for its clear, clean fawn colours with the desired pigmentation – not altogether an easy task. Ch. Oldwell Toby of Studburgh, bred by Mrs D. Butler (sired by Ch. Master Brandy of Marbette out of Miss Polly of Marbette), was particularly remarkable in the stock he produced, including Ch. Yorkist Magician of Oldwell (*see* below) and Ch. Regent of Oldwell. Ch. Regent gained his title in double quick time and was used extensively at stud – as a result, his name appears in the pedigrees of many of today's top-quality dogs.

The Oldwell Kennels of Mr and Mrs Harry Colliass were based originally on Marbette and Buttonoak lines. Mr and Mrs Colliass had already owned some Bullmastiffs in the 1940s, but Harry did not consider them suitable as foundation stock and so purchased Ace of Buttonoak and May Queen of Marbette. From these came Oldwell's first champion, Ch. Bambino of Oldwell. The Colliasses also produced Dilly of Oldwell from their first pair, who was the dam of Ch. Dancer of Oldwell and Ch. Duchess of Oldwell. Ch. Dancer of Oldwell was sired by Ch. Oldwell Mi-Trooper of Marbette, and won the bitch Challenge Certificate at Crufts three years in a row. She was not the biggest of bitches but she certainly made up for it in quality.

Since then there have been at least fifty Oldwell champions, plus many more worldwide, either bred directly at Oldwell or from quality exported stock. Indeed, Harry and Beryl, with the aid of John Swanson, their treasured 'kennel lad', bred many a fine litter. Oldwell dogs were the stock from which the vast majority of dogs, either being shown or being used for breeding, in most of the established kennels in Britain today – including our own. Various combinations of Oldwell dogs and bitches can be relied upon to produce similar types: one particular combination, Ch. Nicholas of Oldwell and St Mungo Minerva, produced no less than seven champions, four in one litter, and as far as we are aware this is still a breed record. No matter where they are in the world, Oldwell dogs can be recognized at a single glance.

Due to old age Harry and Beryl have now handed Oldwell over to their daughter Ann, who has taken it upon herself to become the mainstay of the kennels. Not only does she look after her horses, but she also does most of the work associated with looking after a kennel full of dogs. As she does not have as much time as she would like to attend shows, the dogs are now handled and shown by Mr Billy Brittle, who owned Ch. Oldwell Corrallian.

The 1950s and 1960s

The year 1950 saw the start of the famous Bulstaff Kennels of Ralph and Ruth Short. This kennel later showed with great success Ch. Bulstaff Prudence of Torthorwald; Ch. Bulstaff Brobdignag, sire of Ch. Bulstaff Achilles (still the British breed record-holder, with twenty-six Challenge Certificates, twenty-four of which were gained under different judges); Ch. Bulstaff Leah; Ch. Bulstaff Rosalynde of Ivywill, owned and shown by Bill and Ivy Leedham (Rosalynde was the mother of Mr Leedham's home-bred Ch. Rommel of Ivywill, a dog that had a great influence on future stock in the Northwest and the Midlands); Ch. Bulstaff Topsy; Ch. Bulstaff Revelry; Ch. Bulstaff Heritage of Ellney, owned by Mrs Molly Elliott; Ch. Bulstaff Solomon, owned by Mr C. Nunn; and numerous overseas champions (a great many of the more influential overseas kennels were based on the best of Bulstaff stock).

At this time another very successful kennel, the celebrated Goodstock Kennels of the Misses Edna and Billie Goodhall, was also established. This kennel was based mainly on Rodenhurst stock and the Harecastle line of Miss Lydia Lowe from Kidsgrove. The Goodstock dogs were recognized throughout the breed in the UK as having exceptionally good heads, of correct size and proportions. Some of the outstanding dogs either bred or owned by this kennel were Ch. Goodstock Hunch of Gwydyr, Ch. Goodstock Lord Joyful, Ch. Goodstock Lady Joyful, Ch. Joyous of Goodstock, Ch. Goodstock Joyful Lass, Ch. Goodstock Cherie, Ch. Romper Lad of Goodstock (owned and campaigned by Mrs May Pope), Ch. Goodstock Twinkle-toes (owned by Mrs Molly Segar), Ch. Goodstock Gay Kavalier (owned by Mr and Mrs Monday), and Ch. Goodstock Don Juan (owned in partnership with Mr L. Hirst, who campaigned him to his title as Edna was not in the best of health at that time). Ch. Goodstock Don Juan was later exported to Japan. Ch. Romper Lad of Goodstock gained his title in very quick succession after winning the Challenge Certificate at Crufts in 1961. This dog had an exceptionally large square head of near-perfect proportions and a well-constructed body to match. Unfortunately, he only sired one litter, much to May Pope's disappointment.

For many years Edna Goodhall was Secretary of the Bullmastiff Association, which without her tireless work and efforts, together with those of Chairman Mr W. Burgess of Graystan fame, would most certainly have ceased to exist. Most of the dogs north of the

Midlands being shown or bred from today can be traced back to Goodstock dogs.

A small but select kennels around this time was that of the Yorkist Bullmastiffs founded by Mrs Margaret Reynolds. Margaret was another breeder who specialized in the pale fawn colour, and her more memorable dogs were Ch. Yorkist Minstrel, Ch. Yorkist Magician of Oldwell, Ch. Yorkist Miss Muffet, and Ch. Yorkist Marquis (owned by Mr Hirst). Ch. Yorkist Magician of Oldwell, sired by Ch. Oldwell Toby of Studburgh and bred by Mrs Reynolds, was owned and shown by Harry and Beryl Colliass. He was a good, upstanding, square dog, and although he took a long time to mature, when he did so he was a dog to be reckoned with.

Jim and Dorothy Price of Lombardy fame became actively involved with the breed in the early 1950s, since when they have produced and shown some very good Bullmastiffs, in particular Ch. Harvester of Lombardy, who gained his title in the mid-1960s. This dog's colour was a blast from the past, being a deep deer-red colour with not one hair of any colour other than that called for in the Standard. He had a beautiful head of correct proportion and was always shown in hard muscular condition, with not an ounce of fat anywhere – a real credit to his owners. His son, Ch. Lombardy Simon of Silverfarm, followed in his father's footsteps. He was bred by Mrs Parkes, a true lady in the breed and a good friend of Jim and Dorothy's, who was noted for her brindles – in particular Copper of Silverfarm. A later dog of Mr Price's with the same distinct red colour was Ch. Lombardy Tristam, followed by Ch. Lombardy Harvey and Ch. Lombardy Lewellyn. Jim Price is still very active in the breed today, and continues to both show and breed.

When we (the authors) first met in 1958 Alan already had two unregistered bitches with which we did obedience work. It wasn't until 1960 that we obtained our first Kennel Club registered Bullmastiff, and in the same year we joined the Bullmastiff Association after meeting the then Secretary, Edna Goodhall of the Goodstock Kennels, at the Cheshire Championship Show. Edna sparked off our interest in the showing aspect of the Bullmastiff. After refusing the first two invitations to judge, Alan finally accepted and judged the breed for the first time in 1968, and Mave later judged for her first time in 1972. Due to Alan's reccuring illness we curtailed showing for a number of years, although we continued to breed the odd litter. Some of the more memorable dogs we have had include Ch. Graecia Centaur, Ch. Graecia Celeste, Ch. Saturn of Graecia, Ch.

Graecia Celestine, Ch. Graecia Mercury, Fin. Ch. Graecia Miramba, and Int. Ch. Graecia Rhapsody.

It was in 1959 that the Kelwall Kennels of Lyn and Walter Pratt was started, whose dog Ch. Darrel of Kelwall won the Reserve Best in Show at the 1967 Blackpool Championship Show. Later came Ch. Derry of Kelwall, owned and shown by Mrs Howard and in our opinion a good type of dog. Mrs Pratt is the breed correspondent for Our Dogs magazine, but although they are still judging Walter and Lyn have not been showing or breeding for some years.

Ch. Little Miss of Oldwell, Best of Breed at Crufts 1968, and Bullmastiff of the Year 1968.

Also at this time Doreen and Granville Blount set up the Naukeen Kennels. They had a great deal of success with their dog Goodstock Bash On, unfortunately always the bridesmaid and never the bride, gaining numerous Reserve Challenge Certificates. Their first champion, in 1965, was Ch. Hakmaluk of Naukeen, followed by Ch. Stephan of Naukeen. Then came Ch. Naukeen Lorraine, sired by Ch. Regent of Oldwell out of Ma Belle of Naukeen; this really typical bitch was of a beautiful clear, fawn colour with a good strong, square, black muzzle. Lorraine produced an excellent son by Naukeen Masked Major, namely Ch. Naukeen Ranger. Another good-sized bitch from this kennel was Ch. Naukeen Liela. After this run of champions (the last four gained their titles in the 1970s), the Naukeen Kennels continued to flourish, and in 1985 a bitch belonging to Mrs M. McNaught, Ch. Naukeen Melody Maker of Dreadnot, gained her title. A brindle dog Ch. Naukeen Danial, owned by Mrs Joan Podd, and the really outstanding red dog Ch. Naukeen Major Kew of Eastlynn soon followed. Major Kew was owned by Mrs M. Qualters, who campaigned him successfully to the title of Top Bullmastiff 1986. He was also awarded Best in Show at the Southern Bullmastiff Society's Golden Jubilee Show in 1985 under breed experts Harry and Beryl Colliass of Oldwell fame.

Mr Blount continued showing to success, with Ch. Naukeen Thunder, Ch. Boomerang of Naukeen, and Ch. Naukeen Night Ranger (who was later exported to Australia, where he quickly became an Australian Champion), Ch. Naukeen Heath Thyme, Ch. Naukeen Morag of Dreadnot (owned and shown by Mrs McNaught), and, last but not least, Ch. Naukeen Sweet Poppet.

Mrs Joyce James of the Morejoy prefix arrived on the scene in the late 1950s. Her more memorable dogs were Ch. Morejoy Pride Amanda, born in 1961, followed by Ch. Morejoy Eastern Princess, a really top-quality red bitch. Mrs James is still active in the breed today and is currently President of the Welsh and West of England Bullmastiff Society. Her son, Dr Ronald James, is Chairman of the same club and is an active member of the Breed Council.

Mr and Mrs Jim Leeson, who had previously owned and bred Bull-Terriers, obtained their first Bullmastiff from the Naukeen Kennels of Mr and Mrs Blount in 1968. She was registered as Lady Cleopatra of Naukeen, bred by Miss E. B. Chamberlaine. This bitch was mated to Bulstaff Turvey to produce Mr and Mrs Leeson's Ch. Pitmans Gentleman Jim, while out of Jim's litter-sister, Pitmans Lady Dorothea, by Ch. Bulstaff Revelry came Ch. Pitmans Sir Albert, owned by Mr Pick. This dog was an outstanding specimen of the breed but unfortunately, to our knowledge, never sired a litter. Later came Ch. Pitmans Buccaneer (sired by Ch. Craigylea Sir Galahad), Ch. Pitmans Deputy, and Ch. Sharwell Mean Mr Mustard of Pitmans (bred by Mr and Mrs K. Bakewell). When he appeared on the scene Mean Mr Mustard gave a much-needed boost to Bullmastiffs in the UK in terms of height, as apart from a few exceptions many dogs were not as tall as they should be.

The Bullmastiff Breed Council   The inauguration of the Bullmastiff Breed Council of the United Kingdom took place in 1968. Breed councils were formed at the suggestion of The Kennel Club, the idea behind their formation being that they would liaise between the breed clubs and The Kennel Club. The Bullmastiff Breed Council is composed of four elected delegates from each of the constituent clubs. Its aims are to discuss all matters relating to the Bullmastiff, and to compile judges' lists as per Kennel Club recommendations

Ch. Copperfield Sarah Pocket, Bullmastiff of the Year 1972.

and to furnish show secretaries with such lists as applicable. The Council organizes and conducts seminars on such subjects as health, judging, breeding, ethics and the law, and general education, together with any reasonable subject proposed by a constituent club. At this time of writing the Council was also engaged in a feasibility study into the possibility of commissioning a video film to explain the requirements of the Breed Standard.

The constituent clubs of the Council today are the British Bullmastiff League, the Bullmastiff Association, the Southern Bullmastiff Society, the Welsh and West of England Bullmastiff Society, and the Bullmastiff Society of Scotland. All the constituent clubs are entitled to refer any matter they may choose concerning Bullmastiffs to the Breed Council for discussion.

The 1970s

The early 1970s saw the arrival of Mr and Mrs Bill Newton with the prefix Craigylea. The best-known dog with this prefix was Ch. Craigylea Sir Galahad. He was born in 1974, and at Crufts in 1977 he won the dog Challenge Certificate, Best in Breed, and then went on to win the Working group. In 1978 and 1979 he won the Challenge Certificate. Owing to an unfortunate oversight, Mr Newton later lost the right to use the prefix Craigylea, but some years later registered the prefix Galastock. In 1986 a mating of Mr Newton's Galastock Victoria to Ch. Sharwell Mean Mr Mustard of Pitmans produced Ch. Galastock Danny Boy, together with his brother Ch. Galastock Sonny Boy (owned by Mr J. Newton) and sister Ch. Galastock Sugar and Spice. A fourth dog from this litter, Galastock Mr Todd, owned and shown by Mr C. Newton, won one Challenge Certificate. Ch. Danny Boy and Ch. Sugar and Spice were an exceptional pair and a credit both to the breed and their breeders.

Bill and Fran Harris of the Bunsoro prefix obtained their first Bullmastiff in 1971, since when they have consistently shown dogs that have done well in the ring. In particular these include Ch. Bunsoro Penny Lane, Ch. Maggie May of Bunsoro (bred by Mr Tom Massey, and in our opinion one of the best bitches in the breed for a good number of years), and Ch. Bunsoro Bombadier. More recently the Harrises have bred or shown various champions, culminating in Ch. Bunsoro Red Sails.

It was in 1972 that the Bullmastiff Society of Scotland was formed, the fifth Bullmastiff club in the UK.

Also in 1972 Mrs W. M. Cox of the Colom prefix obtained her original bitch, Lombardy Rosamunda, from Mr and Mrs Jim Price. This bitch was mated to Ch. Lombardy Simon of Silverfarm, and in July 1974 Ch. Colom Florin, an exceptional-quality bitch of a deep, rich red colour, was born. In April 1978 Ch. Colom Florin's litter by Ch. Naukeen Ranger was born. From this litter came Ch. Colom Nellie and Ch. Colom Jumbo, who went on to win the Working group at the Blackpool Championship Show in 1981. In 1985 Mrs Cox won the Challenge Certificate and Best in Breed at Crufts with Ch. Ivywill Wagga Wagga of Colom, bred by Bill and Ivy Leedham.

Mr Crawford Taylor founded the Bryany Bullmastiff Kennels of Perth, Scotland, in 1973. His first champion was the brindle bitch Ch. Rima Renoun, followed by Ch. Bryany Brunette (owned by Captain and Mrs Goodlad), Ch. Bryany Bullet, Ch. Bryany Starboy, and Ch. Bryany Claudette.

On 13 July 1975 a championship show organized jointly by the bullmastiff clubs was held to celebrate the golden jubilee of the breed's Kennel Club recognition; it was held at the National Agricultural Centre, Stoneleigh. The renowned international judge, the late Mr R. M. James, was invited to judge the show, and the event drew a then record entry of 161 dogs from all corners of the UK. Mr James found his Best in Show winner in Mr and Mrs Leeson's Ch. Pitmans Gentleman Jim, sired by Bulstaff Turvey out of Lady Cleopatra of Naukeen. The bitch Challenge Certificate and Best Opposite Sex was awarded to Mr and Mrs Lowrie's Ch. Leyrigg Rhinestone Ruby, sired by Azer of Oldwell out of Damaron Aristo Gold. Best Puppy in Show went to Mr and Mrs Price's Lombardy Raffles, sired by Ch. Lombardy Tristram out of Lombardy Marcella.

Also in 1975 Mr Tom Massey established his Todomas Kennels with his foundation bitch Sackville Princess. She was mated to Ch. Bunsoro Cloudburst and from this one litter produced Ch. Maggie May of Bunsoro, Ch. Bombadillo of Bunsoro, and Ch. Todomas Duchess. Later, Tom bred the really exceptional bitch Ch. Todomas Tamar, who for a number of years held the breed record for the highest number of Challenge Certificates won by a bitch. Another of Tom's great successes was Ch. Todomas Yvonne, a brindle bitch handled and shown by his son, Mr A. Massey.

The Cadenham Kennels of Daphne Peglar and her daughter Felicity was founded in 1977. They owned and actively campaigned the well-known bitch Ch. Coomberlain River Worle, who became their first champion and well deserved her title. Later they bred the

Ch. Jagopeeko Bold Borage.

grand, pale fawn dog Ch. Cadenham Ben Gunn, then came Ch. Filand Man of Harlech at Cadenham and, more recently, Ch. Cadenham Blonde Ambition (owned by Mr and Mrs Seger). This bitch was handled and fearlessly campaigned by Felicity throughout the year and went on to win Bullmastiff of the Year 1994. She later went to the USA where she soon became an American champion.

The early days of Wally and May Scott of the Lepsco Bullmastiffs will always be remembered for their bitch Lin Toosey. In later years they bred the bitch Ch. Lepsco Lady Elise of Flintstock, owned and campaigned by Janet and Alec Gunn, which won the bitch Challenge Certificate at Crufts in 1992.

Also in the late 1970s came the Dajean Kennels of Shelly Thomsett, née Woods. This kennel had won a Challenge Certificate and a couple of Reserves, when in 1990 the young bitch Dajean Golden Autocrat was mated to Ch. Saturn of Graecia. From this litter she produced Ch. Dajean Red Dragon, owned and campaigned by Mr G. Slater. This dog went on to win numerous Challenge Certificates and had multiple Working group wins. His litter-sister, Ch. Dajean Golddust the Poachersfoe, owned and shown fearlessly by Jaquie and Ged Ling, became the top-winning bitch of all time, taking a total of twenty-one Challenge Certificates, including Crufts.

John and Sue Reynolds started their Tartuffe Kennel in 1979. When they showed their foundation bitch at their first Bullmastiff club show, they were told by older breeders that she lacked expression, was too fat, and simply wouldn't do well. Sue, not being easily discouraged and always an optimist, later mated her to Ch. Pitmans Deputy, and from this mating she produced for them their first

*Mrs Higginson of Stanfell Kennels judging Ch. Bulstaff Achilles
(left, with Mr Ralph Short) and Ch. Miss Oldwell (with Mr Harry
Colliass).*

champion, Ch. Tartuffe Priam. From another bitch of theirs they
then produced Ch. Tartuffe Arachne and Ch. Tartuffe Apollo. They
subsequently bred a really promising red dog, Tartuffe Red Baron,
which tragically was killed in a road accident. They later acquired an
outstanding fawn dog, Rakwana Oberon of Tartuffe (bred by Mrs
Chapple), whom they campaigned to his title. Sue has recently
started showing another young dog, Tartuffe Revelry, who has so
far won two Challenge Certificates – no doubt it won't be too long
before he gets his third.

Oldwell stayed ahead in terms of the number of champions bred
or shown, with Bulstaff, Copperfield, and Naukeen following. The
most exceptional dogs from these and other kennels shown during
the 1970s include Ch. Oldwell Queen Gweniveve of Muraken, Ch.
Honey Bee of Oldwell, Ch. Frazer of Oldwell, Ch. Bulstaff Revelry,

*Ch. Saturn of Graecia. Best of Breed Crufts 1989, and Top Sire UK
from 1992 to 1995.*

Ch. Copperfield Sarah Pocket, Ch. Naukeen Lorraine, Ch. Pitmans
Sir Albert, Ch. Pekintown Abece, Ch. Lombardy Simon of Silverfarm,
Ch. Leyrigg Rhinestone Ruby, Ch. Bunsoro Penny Lane, Ch.
Craigylea Sir Galahad, and Ch. Maggie May of Bunsoro.

The 1980s

The 1980s saw the formation of the Jagopeeko Bullmastiffs of Ewart
and Jenny Grant, based very much on the Oldwell type of dog.

Ch. Dajean Golddust the Poachersfoe and her daughter, Poachersfoe Prudence.

Ewart's first bitch was Gypsy Jag of Peeko. Sadly, Jenny passed away shortly after the kennel had become firmly established and had started to produce top-quality winning stock. Much later Ewart met and married Sally, who had been involved with Bullmastiffs for quite some time, and thus their current partnership began. Some of their more memorable dogs were Ch. Jagopeeko Inara, her brother, Ch. Jagopeeko Inam of Oldwell (owned by Mr Colliass), Ch. Jagopeeko Bordacea, Ch. Bold Borage Jagopeeko, and, more recently, Ch. Jagopeeko Wood Sorrel.

Malcolm and Angie McInnes became involved with Bullmastiffs in 1982. They worked hard at their breeding programme for a number of years and were rewarded with Ch. Morvern Elyse and, later, with Ch. Morvern Grenadier. They bred and exported the young red dog Morvern Eachern to Australia, where he later became an Australian champion.

32

Ch. Lepsco Lady Elise of Flintstock.

Colin and Mary Jones's Maxstoke Kennel was founded in 1982, based upon Naukeen and Colom lines. In 1987 Ch. Maxstoke Bassey, a neat red bitch, became their first champion, soon followed by another good champion, Ch. Maxstoke Elkie, and then Ch. Maxstoke Erwyn. Ch. Maxstoke Elkie took the Challenge Certificate at Crufts twice, once in 1989 and again in 1990 when she also won Best in Breed. At the time of writing Colin and Mary were showing Ch. Maxstoke Monty.

The 1980s witnessed several key events. The Southern Bullmastiff Society held its Golden Jubilee Show in 1985. The judges were Mr and Mrs Colliass, who found their Best in Show in Mrs Marie Qualter's Ch. Naukeen Major Kew of Eastlynn (bred by Mr and Mrs G. Blount). Best Opposite Sex went to Mr E. Grant's home-bred Ch. Jagopeeko Inara. The following year the Bullmastiff Association held its first championship show. The judge on this occasion was Mrs M. Reynolds of Yorkist fame, whose Best in Show was Mr Colliass's Ch. Wyburn Rhula of Oldwell and whose Reserve Best in Show and Best Bitch was our Ch. Graecia Celeste.

The Northern Bullmastiff Club was formed in 1988, becoming the sixth Bullmastiff club in the UK. Also in that year, the first Irish Bullmastiff champion, Mr J. McCartan's Ch. Wrinkles of Leitrim, gained his title. His sire was Clywoods Red Baron and his dam Kizzie Conundrum, and he was bred by D. Keisslinger.

Some of the more exceptional dogs of the decade include the following: Ch. Naukeen Major Kew of Eastlynn, Top Bullmastiff in 1986; Ch. Graecia Celeste Top Bullmastiff Bitch in 1986; Ch. Todomas Tamar, who for a time held the record for the number of Challenge Certificates gained by a bitch; Ch. Graecia Centaur, Best in Breed at Crufts in 1984 and sire of the 1989 winner; Ch. Wyburn Rhula of Oldwell, Best in Breed at Crufts in 1987; Ch. Saturn of Graecia, Best in Breed at Crufts in 1989; Ch. Wyburn Rhian of Oldwell; Ch. Sharwell Mean Mr Mustard of Pitmans; Ch. Galastock Danny Boy; and Ch. Galastock Sugar and Spice.

The All-Winners Event   This event began in 1992, and is an invitation contest to which all the dogs and bitches that have won either a Challenge Certificate or a Reserve Challenge Certificate during the previous year are invited to compete. It is divided into four sections: dogs under four years; dogs over four years; bitches under four years; and bitches over four years. The winners of each of the dog sections are brought together and the judges then decide which is the best of these; this procedure is repeated for the bitch sections. The best dog and bitch then compete for the Best of All Winners.

The winner of the first event was the bitch Ch. Dajean Golddust the Poachersfoe, sired by Ch. Saturn of Graecia out of Dajean Golden Autocrat; she also took the event in the following year. Mr and Mrs Gunn's Ch. Lepsco Lady Elise of Flintstock (sired by Dajean Our Man Flint out of Maxstoke Meggie of Lepsco) took top honours in 1994, while in 1995 Slater and Duke's Ch. Dajean Red Dragon took top

Ch. Wyburn Rhian of Oldwell.

spot; he was sired by Ch. Saturn of Graecia out of Dajean Golden Autocrat. In 1996 the event was not held, but in 1997 top honours went to our Ch. Graecia Mercury (by Ch. Saturn of Graecia out of Graecia Gemini).

The 1990s

Several other important events were held during the 1990s. The Bullmastiff Association held a championship show to celebrate its diamond jubilee in September 1994. The judge was the world-renowned Finnish all-rounder Mr Reiner Vourinen, who drew a

35

record entry for the time with 199 dogs. Best in Show was our Ch. Graecia Mercury, and Reserve Best in Show went to Mr and Mrs Seger's Ch. Cadenham Blonde Ambition (she later returned with her owners to the USA, where she soon became an American champion). Best Puppy was Mr and Mrs Harris's Bunsoro Red Sails.

The Southern Bullmastiff Society held its Diamond Jubilee Championship Show on 6 August 1995 at Leatherhead, Surrey. This show again drew a record entry of 213 exhibits; the appointed judges were breed specialists Mr Gerald Warren (Copperfield) and Mrs Lyn Pratt (Kelwall). Best in Show was Ch. Graecia Mercury, while Reserve Best in Show was Wyburn Hannah.

The Golden Jubilee Show of the Welsh and West of England Bullmastiff Society was held in July 1996. The judge for this occasion was the all-rounder Mrs Pamela Cross-Stern, who found her Best in Show in Mr E. Thompson's Ch. Dixson of the Green; Reserve Best in Show went to Mrs Peglar and Mrs Wilson's Cadenham Bright Spark.

March 1997 saw the Silver Jubilee Championship Show of the Bullmastiff Society of Scotland. The judge on this occasion was the highly respected Mr Andrew Burt from Australia. He found his Best in Show in our Ch. Graecia Mercury; Best Opposite Sex went to Mr and Mrs Bullock's Ch. Bullenca Crystal.

We cannot close this section on the 1990s without mentioning its outstanding dogs. These include Ch. Dajean Golddust the Poachersfoe, Ch. Dajean Red Dragon, Ch. Lepsco Lady Elise of Flintstock, and Ch. Graecia Mercury, all of whom won the All-Winners Event as mentioned above. Also Ch. Saturn of Graecia, Top Sire in 1992, 1993, 1994, and 1995, and Ch. Dixson of the Green, who twice gained Best in Show awards at all-breeds championship shows. Kennels that started to make their impressions in the breed during the decade, and who no doubt will contribute greatly to its future, are Barrus, Bournvalley, Bullenca, Chalfs, Evenstar, Flintstock, Jobulls, Kadcruff, Licassa, Meitza, Murbisa, Parabull, Poachersfoe, Rodekes, Troumaca, Volcalin, and Wherewithall. If these breeders are half as dedicated as those involved in the early development of the breed, then Bullmastiffs must surely have a most secure and promising future in the UK.

2

The Breed Standard

What is a Standard?

In the context of dog breeding a standard is a description which when adhered to will produce a specific type of animal. Standards were initially compiled by people who were interested, enthusiastic, and dedicated to the breed, and were usually agreed after long and careful discussion. The main purpose of any written standard is to enable a person to formulate a reasonable picture of what is required for a typical specimen of that particular breed.

While a standard is considered gospel, it is not carved in granite. So, if a particular point needs to be made more explicit, or if it is found that an aspect of the standard is detrimental, then the standard should be amended accordingly. It is then of paramount importance that the original concept, together with the original purpose for which the breed was developed, should always be kept to the fore.

In our opinion the standard should be so written as to make it difficult for any dog to fulfil all the criteria completely. When standards are so slack or indiscriminate that dogs of widely varying differences are still able to fulfil its requirements, a slow decline in the overall quality of the breed will result.

Early Standards

From the time of the official recognition of the Bullmastiff in 1924 there have been several standards for the breed, usually formulated and agreed by the members of the relevant clubs. At one stage, in 1926, two standards were in force at one time – the Standard of the Midland Bull Mastiff Club and that of the National Bull-Mastiff Police Dog Club. These were followed by the Southern Bullmastiff Society's 1943 Standard, which remained extant until all the parties concerned came to an agreement with the Kennel Club to produce an official Breed Standard in 1950.

In January 1950, the Kennel Club published the following acknowledgements in the *Kennel Club Standards Book*: 'The Committee of the Kennel Club wishes to acknowledge the assistance given by the Breed Representatives of the Kennel Club Liaison Council and the Officials and Committees of the Breed Specialist Clubs in the compiling of these standard descriptions of the breeds.' Apart from minor changes this remained the official Kennel Club Standard until it was revised in 1994.

Due to lack of space we cannot reprint the early standards in full, but are only able to highlight the main differences when comparing them to one another and to the present (1994) Kennel Club Standard.

There are few differences between the first two standards (the Midland Bullmastiff Club Standard and the National Bull-Mastiff Police Dog Club Standard), apart from that of a 1in (2.5cm) disparity in height and ½in (1.2cm) disparity in the length of muzzle. The first standard stresses that a strong muzzle is necessary, whereas in the second this point is not emphasized. There is no mention of colour for the mask in the first standard, but in the second there is a definite preference for a dark mask.

By the time of the 1943 Southern Bullmastiff Society and Training Club Standard, the required heights had been confirmed as 25–27in (64–69cm) for dogs and 24–26in (61–66cm) for bitches. The weights, however, had been increased from 90lb (41kg) and 110lb (50kg) for dogs to 100lb (45kg) and 125lb (57kg), and in bitches from 80lb (36kg) and 90lb (41kg) to 90lb (41kg) and 110lb (50kg) respectively.

In the 1943 Standard the comment 'fair wrinkle when interested, but not in repose' was added to the section referring to the head, which had in the previous standard simply stated 'fair wrinkle'. It was also stressed in 1943 that the muzzle should be cut off blunt and form a right angle with the upper line of the face. With regards to the flews, the words 'not hanging below the level of the bottom of the lower jaw' were added, thus giving a definite assessment as to the maximum length of flews acceptable (this had previously read 'flews not too pendulous'). For the first time the phrase 'Stop definite' was added, as was detail on the size and colour of the ears. The description of feet changed from 'large feet' to 'not large feet'. Crank tails were first recognized as a fault, while it was stated that silky or woolly coats would be penalized and that 'long coats are not eligible for competition'. The fact that long coats were mentioned in particular, along with the change in the number of points allocated for coat, would suggest that there may have been a problem with long coats in the breed at that time. For the first time the colour red was added to the Standard, and the wording 'black mask' was incorporated. A small white mark on the chest was considered permissible, while other white markings were a definite fault. The reference to the tail reaching below the hocks had been removed.

Comparing the 1943 and 1950 standards, the length of muzzle at 3½in (9cm) was deleted from the earlier version, the revised standard requiring the muzzle to be not more than one-third of the length from tip of nose to occiput. The reference to girth and ribs was removed, which unfortunately also took with it the fact that the ribs should extend well back towards the hips. The reference to long coats 'not eligible for competition' had been removed, and the colour of the muzzle was changed from 'black' to 'dark'. 'Dark toenails desirable' was also added at this time. The maximum weight for dogs was increased by 5lb (2kg) from 125lb (57kg) to 130lb (59kg), yet the weights for bitches were left unchanged.

Leading on to the latest Kennel Club Standard (1994), the phrase 'sound and active' was added to the General Appearance section. The wording on the muzzle was changed from 'not more than one third' to 'approximately one third', the long coat was still included, and for the first time in any of the breed's UK standards a section for Gait and Movement was added. All reference to the size of feet was deleted.

The main thing that stands out from these comparisons is the increase in weights. Other noticeable changes include the various lengths of muzzle that have been accepted as correct throughout the years, and the fact that the maximum height for both dogs and bitches has decreased by 1in (2.5cm) at the shoulder from 28in (71cm) to 27in (69cm) for dogs, and from 27in (69cm) to 26in (66cm) for bitches, which is still beyond many present-day bitches being exhibited. Also interesting is the fact that originally the feet had to be large, then the Standard was amended to read 'not large', while at present there is no mention at all of size of feet. A particularly striking fact is that the colour red was not included until 1943. Finally, an example of how personal preferences are imposed on standards can be seen in mask colour, which has alternated from dark to black to dark, and back again to black.

Below are reproduced the UK Breed Standard (1994) and an interpretation of it, and the breed standards from the United States and

Canada (the Australian Breed Standard is the same as that of the UK). It is interesting to compare the UK Standard with those of the US and Canada as the latter two highlight the importance other countries attribute to different aspects of the breed.

The purpose of any standard is to enable the reader to understand the requirements of the breed and to visualize the animal described. Some standards for the Bullmastiff achieve this better than others. On studying and comparing the various standards, it will be noticed that the Canadian Kennel Club's is, to its credit, more explicit than any of the others. The UK Standard, along with some others, contains descriptions that in our opinion are open to misinterpretation. We don't need change for change's sake, but we feel that words such as 'approximate' should be replaced with 'precisely', and 'may' should be replaced with 'should'. As the breed has continued to develop throughout the years, changes have been made to the Standard. For the most part, these changes have been implemented for the betterment, rather than to the detriment, of the Bullmastiff, and we have no doubt that other well-considered changes will continue to take place in the future. The ideal would be an international Standard agreed by all interested parties and implemented world wide, for despite their differences all the standards broadly describe the same dog.

The UK Breed Standard (1994)

(Reproduced by kind permission of the Kennel Club.)

General Appearance

Powerful build, symmetrical, showing great strength, but not cumbersome; sound and active.

Characteristics

Powerful, enduring, active and reliable.

Temperament

High-spirited, alert and faithful.

Head and Skull

Skull large and square, viewed from every angle, fair wrinkle when interested, but not when in repose. Circumference of skull may equal height of dog measured at top of shoulder; broad and deep with well filled cheeks. Pronounced stop. Muzzle short; distance from tip of nose to stop approximately one-third of length from tip of nose to centre of occiput, broad under eyes and sustaining nearly same width to end of nose; blunt and cut off square, forming right angle with upper line of face, and at same time proportionate with skull. Under-jaw broad to end. Nose broad with widely spreading nostrils; flat, neither pointed nor turned up in profile. Flews not pendulous, never hanging below level of lower jaw.

Eyes

Dark or hazel, of medium size, set apart the width of muzzle with furrow between. Light or yellow eyes highly undesirable.

Ears

V-shaped or folded back, set on wide and high, level of occiput giving square appearance to skull which is most important. Small and deeper in colour than body. Point of ear level with eye when alert. Rose ears highly undesirable.

Mouth

Level desired; slightly undershot allowed but not preferred. Canine teeth large and set wide apart, other teeth strong, even and well placed.

Neck

Well arched, moderate length, very muscular and almost equal to skull in circumference.

Forequarters

Chest wide and deep, well let down between forelegs, with deep brisket. Shoulders muscular, sloping and powerful, not overloaded.

41

Forelegs powerful and straight, well boned, set wide apart, presenting a straight front. Pasterns straight and strong.

Body

Back short and straight, giving compact carriage, but not so short as to interfere with activity. Roach and sway backs highly undesirable.

Hindquarters

Loins wide and muscular with fair depth of flank. Hindlegs strong and muscular, with well developed second thighs, denoting power and activity, not cumbersome. Hocks moderately bent. Cow hocks highly undesirable.

Feet

Well arched, cat-like, with rounded toes, pads hard. Dark toenails desirable. Splayed feet highly undesirable.

Tail

Set high, strong at root and tapering, reaching to hocks, carried straight or curved, but not hound-fashion. Crank tails highly undesirable.

Coat

Short and hard, weather-resistant, lying flat to body. Long, silky or woolly coats highly undesirable.

Colour

Any shade of brindle, fawn or red; colour to be pure and clear. A slight white marking on chest permissible. Other white markings undesirable. Black muzzle essential, toning off towards eyes, with dark markings around eyes contributing to expression.

Gait and Movement

Movement indicates power and a sense of purpose. When moving straight neither front nor hindlegs should cross or plait, right front and left rear leg rising and falling at same time. A firm backline unimpaired by powerful thrust from hindlegs denoting a balanced and harmonious movement.

Size and Weight

Height at shoulder: Dogs 63.5–68.5cm (25–27in)
                                  Bitches 61–66cm (24–26in)
Weight: Dogs 50–59kg (110–130lb)
                                  Bitches 41–50 kg (90–110lb).

Faults

Any departure from the foregoing points should be considered a fault, and the seriousness with which the fault should be regarded should be in exact proportion to its degree.

Note
Male animals should have two apparently normal testicles fully descended into the scrotum.

Interpreting the Standard

When studying the Standard, it is important to remember the purpose for which the Bullmastiff was originally developed. It is suggested by the sporting fraternity that the construction of the ancient hound is as near to perfection as one would wish for and, given the purpose for which the hound was bred, we have no reason to doubt this. The construction of any breed of dog is dictated by the breed's original function, so 'perfection' in one type of dog will be undesirable in another whose function is different. The sighthound is long, slender and fairly narrow throughout, with a construction that allows the head to be held on a long neck and well-laid-back shoulders. The Bullmastiff, on the other hand, is robust and heavier than the sighthound in every respect. So if we could produce a Bullmastiff with the desired wide, straight front, well-sprung ribcage, good width of chest and short back, who also possessed the same degree of angulation of a sighthound, built for speed, we would in our opinion have a very exceptional dog. So, as is apparent from this example, it is not necessarily helpful to attempt to draw meaningful comparisons between one breed's construction and another's unless the differences in each breed's function are fully taken into account.

General Appearance

The Bullmastiff should in no way resemble an oversized Bulldog, nor should he give the impression of an undersized Mastiff. The desired general appearance is of a large, well-boned, muscular dog, with a considerable sized square head. He should have a wide front and voluminous ribcage, be fit and athletic-looking, and have strong, well-angulated hindquarters; coupled with this he should show a sparkle for life and have an enthusiasm to please. The overall impression should be of a well-balanced dog with no exaggerations.

Characteristics and Temperament

The desired characteristics and temperament of the Bullmastiff combine high spirits, reliability, activity, endurance, and alertness.

Dealing with high spirits first, in our opinion this means that the dog is happy, amenable, fit, and raring to go. The importance of reliability cannot be overemphasized. The dog must be obedient, pliable, and dependable, with a temperament that is always even. You must be able, without question, to rely on the dog to protect the family members in all situations without his becoming vicious or uncontrollable. Activity, endurance, and alertness all go hand in hand, and refer to a fit, healthy dog that is in hard muscular condition, sound of

Too 'Bulldoggy'.

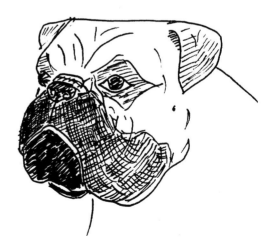

44

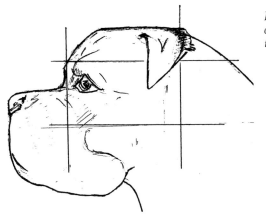

Head proportions: muzzle, one third; stop to occiput, two thirds.

body and mind, and that shows a true eagerness to exercise, work, and play.

As the Bullmastiff was specifically bred to attack on command in defence of his owner, it will take many generations before this type of temperament – considered highly undesirable today – can be completely eradicated from the breed. It is also worth considering whether we should be trying to change the breed too much in this way purely to suit our modern way of life. While we would all prefer an amenable and friendly dog, we should not be too surprised if occasionally one is slightly more aggressive. You cannot blame the dog for his ancestors, and must always remember that at one time a friendly dog would have been frowned upon. That said, you must always ensure that your dog is under complete control at all times.

Head and Skull

The first and most important point we wish to make is that the Bullmastiff does not belong to the brachycephalic group of dogs, nor does he fit into the dolichocephelic group. He does, however, fit much more comfortably into the intermediate mesocephalic group. We would like to emphasize this as there seems to exist a common misconception that the Bullmastiff is a short-faced breed. Examples of short-faced breeds are the Bulldog, Pug, Pekinese, and King Charles Spaniel, to name but a few. The proportions of the Bullmastiff head should in no way equate to those of the breeds mentioned.

We feel it would be advisable for breeders to keep to the Standard's prescribed ratio for muzzle length, which is one third of the length of the head from the tip of the dog's nose to the centre of the occiput. This is important because when you take into account the definite stop, any further shortening of the foreface could result in a shorter, brachycephalic head and the inevitable, assiociated problems of the palate. By keeping the ratio at one-third, the dog is able to grip without suffering breathing difficulties, which was one of the prime functions of the Bullmastiff.

Looking at the skull, the Standard asks for one that is large and square when viewed from every angle. This should be self-explanatory, but unfortunately we still see dogs with narrow, dome-shaped, concave, and completely foreign skulls. We also see some that are large as required, but so shallow from front to back as to be rectangular. The top of the skull should be flat with no apparent indentations of any kind, but it is nevertheless still quite common to see dogs with a V-shaped furrow in the middle of the skull. This is, of course, highly undesirable.

The width of the head depends upon the development and curvature of the zygomatic arch (a bridge of bone connecting the neural and facial areas of the skull). Two of the main facial muscles particularly associated with the Bullmastiff are the temporal and masseter muscles, used for grabbing and holding. The temporal muscle is attached to the sagittal crest and to the surface of the parietal bones. The masseter muscle completely fills the depression below the zygomatic arch and forms the foundation of the cheek. The upper portion is attached to the zygoma and temporal bone; the lower portion is attached to the upright of the mandible. It follows that strong masseter muscles go hand in hand with well-filled cheeks; without well-filled cheeks the muscle is not sufficiently developed and thus cannot grip and hold adequately.

The second line asks for fair wrinkle when interested, but not when in repose. This means exactly what it says: that there should only be wrinkle when the dog is alert and attentive. Unfortunately, it is still quite common to see dogs that are so heavily wrinkled that there is never a time when the head appears free of wrinkle.

The use of the word 'may' in the sentence, 'Circumference of skull may equal height of dog measured at top of shoulder' makes the requirement entirely unclear. In our opinion it would be better to replace 'may' with 'should', or to remove the sentence entirely.

There should be a pronounced stop, forming a near right angle between muzzle and face. Sliding stops and the complete lack of a stop should definitely be penalized. The muzzle should be broad under the eyes and nearly parallel in width, and should be firm and well boned. It should be blunt and cut off square so that a right angle is formed between the end and the upper line of muzzle. The topline of the muzzle must be parallel to the top of the skull when viewed in profile. It is most important that the width, depth, and length of muzzle are in proportion to the skull. Weak and snipey muzzles, and sloping muzzles that give a downfaced expression, should be avoided at all cost.

The underjaw should be broad to the end, and should not resemble the upsweeping underjaw of the Bulldog or Boxer. If the underjaw is more than slightly undershot it will tend to protrude past the level of the nose; in no way can this be interpreted as giving the blunt and square appearance required by the Standard. The nose should be flat and broad with widely spreading nostrils. It must not be upturned so that it breaks the upper line of the muzzle. The flews should not be pendulous as this tends to give the head a wet and droopy appearance, rather like the look of a Bloodhound. They should, however, be neat and clean.

Eyes

Eyes should be dark or hazel; any colour lighter than hazel should be regarded as a fault, the severity of which is at the discretion of the judge. The Standard asks for eyes of medium size, but it must always be borne in mind that they should be in proportion to the size of the head. The current Standard unfortunately makes no mention of the shape or set of eye, only position, which should be the width of the muzzle apart with a furrow between them. We believe that the eye should be almond-shaped and moderately set. Round or bulbous eyes do not give the correct expression and are completely wrong for a Bullmastiff.

Ears

The Standard demands ears that are V-shaped or folded back. This should be straightforward, but as it still appears to lead to many different interpretations perhaps the wording needs to be made more explicit. Ears can either make or break a promising head. Carried correctly they give balance to a somewhat good but narrow skull by accentuating the desired width. Conversely, badly carried ears can detract greatly from a skull that has good width.

The ears should be carried V-shaped and high, the top of the ear forming a continual line with the top of the skull. We believe the point of the ear should be level with the eye when the dog is alert, contrary to the feelings of many exhibitors. Although ears that are folded forward do tend to accentuate the square appearance of the head, it is however perfectly acceptable for them to be folded back, and dogs with such carriage should not be penalized because of it.

The ears should be small, and deeper in colour than the body. This means exactly what it says: that they must be darker than the body colour, but not necessarily black as some people insist. Rose-ears, semi-rose ears, and ears that are carried away from the head are incorrect.

Mouth

The mouth should be level, although a slightly undershot mouth is allowed. Taken literally, this means that the cutting edges of the incisors should meet edge to edge, but as this would be an extremely weak mouth construction it would be far better to stipulate a reverse scissor bite instead. We feel it is much more important to have a wide underjaw, with large, strong, regular teeth, that is slightly undershot, than a level bite in a weak jaw. This would give a far stronger bite that is more capable of gripping.

It is a natural tendency in the mesocephalic breeds for the upper jaw to be slightly shorter than the lower mandible. Breeders should be aware that the requirement asking for a shorter foreface combined with the demand for a level bite contradict the natural way of things. Breeders should therefore pay due attention to these requisites, but should not do so at the expense of the true Bullmastiff expression. Overshot jaws, grossly undershot jaws, narrow underjaws, irregular teeth, and wry jaws in particular are to be avoided.

Neck

A neck of moderate length that is well arched not only looks well balanced but is more efficient. The apparent length of neck depends considerably on the layback of the shoulder. The shoulder muscles are connected to each side of the atlas and axis vertebrae at the crest of the neck and at the lower end to the upper foreleg, and assist in advancing the leg. The cervical ligament provides a stable base for the attachment of the muscles used in moving the leg forward. This would suggest that better control of front movement is obtained if the dog has good muscular neck development. Short necks tend to reduce the length of muscles controlling the shoulder blades, with an accompanying lack of reach in forward movement.

The shorter neck should be avoided at all cost; this consistently demonstrates lack of balance and incorrect angulation between shoulders, neck, and head carriage. Invariably, short necks are an indication of steep/upright shoulders. It is not uncommon to see the head of a dog with this type of neck, when on the move, to go far below the level of the shoulders and the topline to rise towards the hindquarters. One can only assume the dog moves in this way to try to counterbalance the incorrect angulation of the shoulders and assembly of the forequarters.

Forequarters

The chest should not only be wide with great depth, but it should in the adult dog be approximately equal to the full span of a man's hand. The prosternum should, in the soundly constructed dog, be well forward of the front leg, and the depth of brisket must reach down level with the elbows. The forelegs when viewed from the front or in profile should be well boned, straight, strong, and true, with elbows neatly tucked in, and should show no weakness in pasterns.

Unfortunately, far too often one sees dogs with narrow fronts and what little chests they have behind the front legs. When these characteristics are combined with a shallow brisket the result is a gothic arch or inverted 'U', as it is sometimes referred to in the UK. This type of front is definitely not to be encouraged in the Bullmastiff. The distance from the ground to the elbow should be half that between the ground and the point of shoulder (the uppermost point of the scapula). Too often dogs show well-developed ribs with a good depth of brisket, but unfortunately short forelegs that destroy the balance.

Particular attention must be paid to the shoulders, as in producing wide fronts together with straight legs there is a natural tendency for the scapula to be more upright and then to become overloaded to compensate. It is quite common in dogs with too great a distance between the forelegs for the legs to turn outwards, usually from the pastern; this is referred to as an east–west stance.

The angle formed between the scapula and the horizontal should be approximately 50 degrees, and the angle formed between the scapula and the humerus approximately 100 degrees. In order to maintain overall balance, the top of the scapula must be level with the spine, not higher than it. Space between the scapulae helps to produce a good spring of rib while at the same time keeping the front limbs straight and parallel.

Correctly angulated shoulders will allow an upright head carriage, which in turn will encourage the muscles responsible for advancing the forelimb to contract with full advantage. A shoulder that is insufficiently laid back usually goes hand in hand with a head that is carried horizontally with the topline, rather than above it as it should be. In our experience, an upright shoulder coupled with a short neck will force the head carriage even lower so that the head drops down far below the level of the topline; this lowering of the head appears to be the only way the dog can move without rolling the head from side to side.

A common fault with the front assembly in some Bullmastiffs is a humerus that is too short. This severely restricts the length of stride, even when the dog has a well-laid-back shoulder. A shoulder of insufficient inclination can cause the elbows to be forced out-wards, which results in a loose, unsound front.

To summarize, a correctly assembled forequarter, with scapula and humerus of similar length, will give good reach and efficiency of movement.

Body

There should be a well-sprung but not barrelled ribcage. As mentioned above, the brisket should reach down to the elbow. The longer the rib, the deeper the chest and the greater the degree of curvature of the ribs, the greater will be the chest's volume. The ribs should reach well back along the length of the body – obviously, this will make more room for the internal organs.

The back should be short and straight, giving a level topline. It should definitely not rise over the loins. Although some breeders and judges have stated that they prefer bitches to have long backs so that they have more room for carrying whelps, this is an unfounded assumption. Many short-backed breeds – such as Dobermans, Belgian Shepherds, Boxers, and Old English Sheepdogs – produce

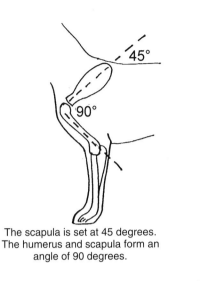

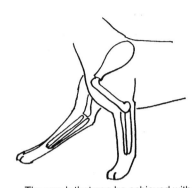

The scapula is set at 45 degrees. The humerus and scapula form an angle of 90 degrees.

The reach that can be achieved with 45/90-degree angulation.

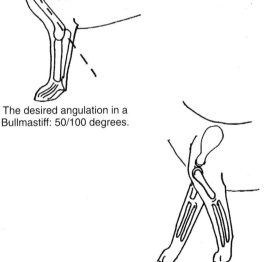

The desired angulation in a Bullmastiff: 50/100 degrees.

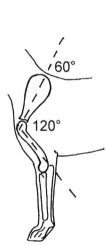

An upright, or steep, shoulder is created by 60/120-degree

Restricted reach, caused by an upright shoulder.

Angulation of the shoulder.

good-sized litters with no particular problems. It is also wrong to differentiate between the sexes in this way as you cannot expect to
breed short-backed dogs from long-backed bitches.

Hindquarters

The hindquarters must be strong, muscular and powerful, with no
exaggerations. A good width of loin is highly desirable. It is completely wrong for a dog to have a weak, narrow loin. A dog with such
a loin and a reasonable ribcage would appear pear-shaped like a
Bulldog when viewed from above, which is highly undesirable.

It is essential that there is good angulation of the hindquarters.
These form the powerhouse of the Bullmastiff, with most propulsion
coming from well-flexed stifles and hocks. The dog needs to get the
hind foot well under the body so that he can propel himself forward,
but he will not be able to do so efficiently without the correct angulation. Remember always that the Bullmastiff was developed as a
working dog and so must be capable of running over difficult terrain
and jumping any obstacles in his way. A dog with the required flexi-
bility of the hindquarters and correct angulation, derived from having
a correctly positioned and angulated pelvis together with a good bend
of stifle and moderately bent hocks, will be able to manage all of this
without placing undue stress and strain on the hindquarters.

As the Bullmastiff is a short-backed breed, the optimum angle
between the pelvis and the horizontal must be approximately 25 to 30
degrees. Too steep an angle of the pelvis can result in overangulated
hindquarters. Such a construction will cause loss of power and drive
as the dog will be unable to achieve the required swing of the
hindquarters. On the other hand, too shallow an angle of the pelvis
will result in most of the propulsion being utilized in lifting the hip
instead of driving the dog forward.

We are in danger of allowing straight stifles to become the norm.
The possibility is all too obvious when one observes the large number of dogs exhibited today that show this fault. The extra strain this
places on the stifle (knee-joint) can cause a great deal of instability. A
fault that is commonly apparent in dogs with straight stifles is sometimes referred to as an inverted hock: instead of the moderate bend
required the configuration of the hock joint is almost 180 degrees. In
severe instances it can go further and form a reflex angle. The instability of the knee joint together with the excess strain caused by the
incorrect hock joint can lead to severe problems, such as the rupture

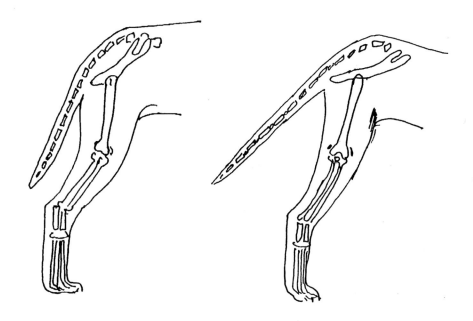

Degrees of straightness in stifle.

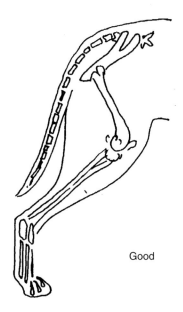

Good

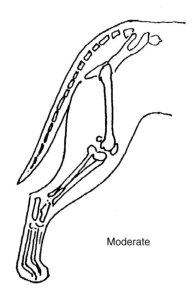

Moderate

Degrees of bend in stifle.

of the cruciate ligament. In any case, unsoundness of the rear quarters is quite common in the dog with straight stifles.

Over-angulation of the stifle usually occurs when the tibia and fibula are too long in comparison to the femur. Exaggerated tibia length can lead to weakness and loose movement – an example of which is 'crabbing', when the dog's body is carried at an angle instead of parallel to the line of travel. Such a dog must swing the hindquarters out of line in order that the hind legs do not interfere with the front ones. We must also mention that careless handling can also create the same effect.

Hocks should be set low, and there should be moderate angulation of the hock joint: when viewed from the rear the hock should be perpendicular to the ground.

Finally, well-developed musculature is essential, for no matter how correctly angulated the hindquarters are they will not be able to fulfil their role efficiently if the muscles are weak.

Feet

A good indication that a dog has good feet is short claws. Long claws can denote toes that do not strike the ground correctly, perhaps for medical reasons or a lack of exercise. Overweight dogs that are exercised and kept on a hard, smooth surface such as concrete can develop splayed feet, which are highly undesirable. Long toes can also cause the foot to appear overlarge. Correct genetic make-up combined with exercise on as many variable surfaces as possible, is conducive to the formation of good feet.

Tail

The length of the tail should reach down to the hock, level with an imaginary line drawn between the two hocks. It should never be carried above the level of the back. If the tail is carried almost vertical at an angle of 90 degrees to the back, this could indicate an incorrectly angulated pelvis. However you view it, such a tail carriage is definitely undesirable, as are crank tails.

Coat

This section of the Standard is completely self-explanatory. The length of coat should not be so long as to have the tendency to be wavy. Remember that the dog was developed to work in cold, wet conditions and so should have a weatherproof coat.

Colour

There are three main points about colour:

1. *Black coloration.* The muzzle together with the nose must be black, toning off towards the eyes. This means that you should be able to see small parts of the body colour between the muzzle and the black rings around the eyes. The black colour should not continue any further up the head than the markings around the eyes. It is important that the shading should not progress beyond the level of the eyes as this will give the head a dirty appearance. It is of equal importance that the muzzle and rings around the eyes do not lack pigment. The claws should be black. Dogs with black markings other than those described are incorrect.
2. *White markings.* It is permissible but not desirable to have a small white mark on the chest, small being the operative word here – no greater than 1¼in (3cm). A white mark on the chest that is in excess of 1¼in (3cm) or that appears anywhere other than on the chest is highly undesirable.
3. *Two-toning.* It is unfortunately becoming more common to see red dogs with a much lighter underside and fawn dogs with almost white undersides, as well as dogs of both colours with black undersides. The colour should be clear and pure throughout the body.

Gait and Movement

When the dog is viewed from the front, there should be no paddling action, the legs should move nearly parallel to each other, and then as speed increases the legs should begin to converge slightly. It is highly undesirable to see the legs converging so far as to be single-tracking or, worse still, crossing. The head carriage should not be lower than the level of the back, but preferably carried higher to give better balance. The hind legs should also move nearly parallel. They should not toe in when the dog is moved at the correct speed, and definitely should not be so close as to touch each other or, worse still, cross. The hocks should be firm and straight, and should display no sideways movement.

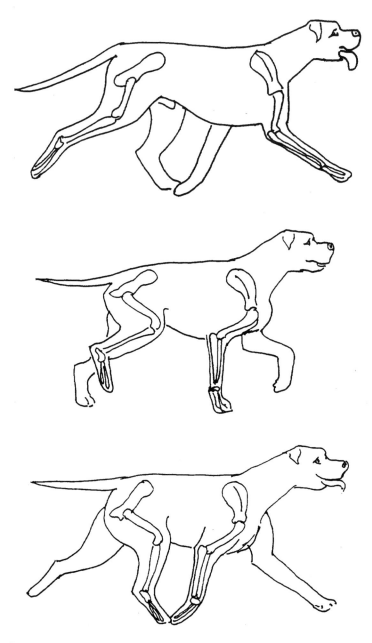

Good movement can be achieved only when the hock and stifle joints flex sufficiently to bring the hind leg well under the body. The ability to extend the legs with power is derived from a well-developed second thigh and correctly inclined pelvis.

The correct gait: the limbs are moved diagonally.

Pacing: the limbs are moved unilaterally.

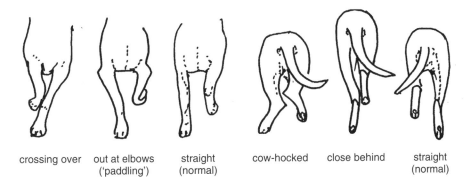

crossing over   out at elbows   straight   cow-hocked   close behind   straight
            ('paddling')   (normal)   (normal)

Front and rear action,

What is commonly but incorrectly termed as 'too long in hock' (meaning that the hock joint is set too high), can lead to unsoundness in movement. When assessing rear movement there is little that looks worse than hocks flapping about loosely when the dog is on the move or hocks moving so close that they actually touch each other. A good, firm, low-set hock allows the dog to flex and drive with power.

A gay tail can be a sign of an insufficient degree of inclination of the pelvis and would usually be accompanied by a stilted rear action, the hind limbs having great difficulty in flexing sufficiently to allow the hind-quarters to reach under the body, thus enabling affective drive.

When viewed in profile, there should be good extension of the forelegs. The stifle and hock should flex sufficiently to allow the rear foot to land approximately in line with the centre of the body. If the hind legs cannot function in this way they will give very little drive.

Balanced and free flowing movement is attained only when there is complete harmony between correctly angulated front and rear quarters. It is apparent when each limb is able to take the correct length of stride and so enable each foot to strike the ground at exactly the correct moment.

Size and Weight

There are definite height and weight sizes set out in the Standard. These must be relative to each other, so that a dog at the lower end of the height scale should weigh at the lower end of the weight scale in order to be balanced, and vice versa.

American Breed Standard

(Reproduced by kind permission of the American Kennel Club.)

General Appearance

That of a symmetrical animal, showing great strength, endurance, and alertness; powerfully built but active. The foundation breeding was 60 per cent Mastiff and 40 per cent Bulldog. The breed was developed in England by gamekeepers for protection against poachers.

Size, Proportion, and Substance

Size: Dogs, 25 to 27 inches at the withers, and 110 to 130 pounds weight. Bitches, 24 to 26 inches at the withers, and 100 to 120 pounds weight. Other things being equal, the more substantial dog within these limits is favoured.
Proportion: The length from tip of breastbone to rear of thigh exceeds the height from withers to ground only slightly, resulting in a nearly square appearance.

Head

Expression: Keen, alert, and intelligent. *Eyes:* Dark and of medium size. *Ears:* V-shaped and carried close to the cheeks, set on wide and high, level with occiput and cheeks, giving a square appearance to the skull; darker in colour than the body and medium in size. *Skull:* Large, with fair amount of wrinkle when alert; broad, with cheeks well developed. Forehead flat. *Stop:* Moderate. *Muzzle:* Broad and deep; its length, in comparison with that of the entire head, approximately as 1 is to 3. Lack of foreface with nostrils set on top of muzzle is a reversion to the Bulldog and is very undesirable. A dark muzzle is preferable. *Nose:* Black, with nostrils large and broad. *Flews:* Not too pendulous. *Bite:* Preferably level or slightly undershot. Canine teeth large and set wide apart.

Neck, Topline, and Body

Neck: Slightly arched, of moderate length, very muscular, and almost equal in circumference to the skull. *Topline:* Straight and level between withers and loin. *Body:* Compact, chest wide and deep, with ribs well sprung and well set down between the forelegs.

Back

Short, giving the impression of a well balanced dog.

Loin

Wide, muscular, and slightly arched with fair depth of flank.

Tail

Set on high, strong at the root, and tapering to the hocks. It may be straight or curved, but never carried hound fashion.

Forequarters

Shoulders muscular but not loaded, and slightly sloping. Forelegs straight, well boned, and set wide apart; elbows turned neither in nor out. Pasterns straight, feet of medium size, with round toes well arched. Pads thick and tough, nails black.

Hindquarters

Broad and muscular, with well developed second thigh denoting power, but not cumbersome. Moderate angulation at hocks. Cow-hocks and splay feet are serious faults.

Coat

Short and dense, giving good weather protection.

Colour

Red, fawn, or brindle. Except for a very small white spot on the chest, white marking is considered a fault.

Gait

Free, smooth, and powerful. When viewed from the side, reach and drive indicate maximum use of the dog's moderate angulation. Back remains level and firm. Coming and going, the dog moves in a straight line. Feet tend to converge under the body, without crossing over, as speed increases. There is no twisting in or out at the joints.

Temperament

Fearless and confident yet docile. The dog combines the reliability, intelligence, and willingness to please required in a dependable family companion and protector.

Canadian Breed Standard

(Reproduced by kind permission of the Canadian Kennel Club.)

Note

Faults are classified as Serious or Minor, indicated as (S) and (M) respectively. Note that MINOR faults are either points which would not of themselves contribute to unsoundness in the dog, or are the result of poor conditioning, which might be controlled, and are not likely to be hereditary.

Origin and Purpose

The Bullmastiff was developed in England by gamekeepers for protection against poachers. The foundation breeding of the modern pure-bred was 60 per cent Mastiff and 40 per cent Bulldog. It is a guard and companion dog, and should be loyal, obedient and thus suitable for training.

General Appearance

The Bullmastiff is a powerfully built, symmetrical dog, showing great strength and activity, but not cumbersome; upstanding and compact in appearance, with breadth and depth of skull and body, the latter set on strong, sturdy, well boned legs. The height measured vertically from the ground to the highest point of the withers should nearly equal the length measured horizontally from the forechest to the rear part of the upper thigh, and should slightly exceed the height at the hips. Bitches are feminine in appearance, of somewhat lighter bone structure than the male, but should still convey strength. Faults: (S) Lack of balance. Poor or light bone structure. (M) Lack of muscular development. Ranginess.

Temperament

The Bullmastiff should be bold, fearless and courageous, a dependable guard dog; alert and intelligent. Faults: (S) Viciousness. Shyness (such dogs should not be used for breeding). (M) Apathy and sluggishness.

Size

Height at the highest point of the withers, dogs, 25 to 27in (63–69cm), bitches, 24 to 26in (61–66cm).

Weight

Dogs, 110 to 130lb (50–59kg); bitches, 100 to 120lb (45–55kg). It is important that weight be in proportion to height and bone structure, to ensure balance. Faults: (S) Over maximum height. Under minimum height. (M) Over maximum weight. Under minimum weight.

Coat and Colour

Short and dense, giving good weather protection. Faults: (S) Long, soft coat. (M) 'Staring' coat, which means poor condition. Colour: Any shade of red, fawn or brindle, but the colour to be pure and clear. A small white marking on chest permissible but not desirable. Faults: (S) White markings other than on chest. (M) Black shading on body, legs or tail (of reds or fawns).

Head

The skull should be large, equal in breadth, length and depth, with a fair amount of wrinkle when the dog is interested; well developed cheeks. The skull in circumference may measure the height of the dog. Forehead flat, with furrow between the eyes. Stop definite. Faults: (S) Narrow skull. Shallow skull. (M) Domed forehead. Insufficient stop. Muzzle should be short, broad and deep, in the same proportions as the skull. The distance from the tip of the nose to the stop should not exceed one third of the length from the tip of the nose to the centre of the occiput. Broad under the eyes and nearly parallel in width to the end of the nose; blunt and cut off square, appearing in profile in a plane parallel to the line of the skull. A black mask is essential. The nose should be black; flat; and broad with widely spreading nostrils when viewed from the front. Flews not too pendulous. The lower jaw broad. Faults: (S) Muzzle too long, too narrow, pointed or lacking in depth. Muzzle too short; nostrils set on top; nose pointed, upturned or laid back; lower jaw narrow. (M) Lack of wrinkle; flews too pendulous. Teeth preferably level bite or slightly undershot. Canine teeth large and set wide apart; other teeth strong, even and well placed. Faults: (S) Teeth overshot. Teeth more than ¼in (0.6cm) undershot. Wry mouth. (M) Irregular or poorly placed teeth. Small teeth. Eyes dark or hazel, and of medium size; set apart the width of the muzzle. Faults: (M) Light eyes. Eyes too close together, too large, too small. Ears V-shaped and carried close to the cheeks; set on wide and high, level with the occiput, giving a square appearance to the skull which is most important. They should be darker in colour than the body, and the point of the ear, when alert, should be level with the eye. Faults: (S) Rose ears. (M) Ears too long or too short. Lack of darker colour.

Neck

Well arched, of moderate length, very muscular, and almost equal in circumference to the skull. Faults: (S) Neck too short; too long. Neck weak and scrawny.

Forequarters

Proper angulation and proportionate bone length of the forequarters are very important. The shoulder bone should slope forward and downwards from the withers at an angle of 45 degrees from the vertical. The humerus (upper arm) should form a right angle with the shoulder bone, 45 degrees from the vertical. The shoulder bone and humerus should be approximately equal in length. The length of the foreleg from the ground to the elbow should be a little more than half the distance from the ground to the withers, approximately 52 per cent. The shoulders and upper arms should be muscular and powerful, but not overloaded. Forelegs powerful, with round heavy bone, vertical and parallel to each other, set well apart; elbows set close to the body; pasterns straight and strong. Feet of medium size, not turning in or out, with round toes, well arched. Pads thick and tough. Nails black. Faults: (S) Lack of proportion in bone. Shoulders too steep. Shoulders overloaded. Elbows turned in or out. Lack of bone in forelegs. Forelegs bowed. Weak pasterns. Splay feet. (M) Feet turned in or out. White nails.

Body and Tail

Body compact. Chest wide and deep, with ribs well sprung and well set down between the forelegs. Back short and level. Loins wide, muscular; croup slightly arched, with fair depth of flank. Faults: (S) Body too long. Shallow chest. Narrow chest. Lack of rib-spring. Sway back. Roach back. Tip of hip bone higher than withers. (M) Too much tuck-up.

Tail set on high, strong at the root and tapering to the hocks. It may be carried straight or curved. Faults: (S) Screw tail. Crank tail. Tail set too low. (M) Tail carried hound fashion. Too long. Too short. Too heavily coated.

Hindquarters

It is important that structure, angulation and proportionate bone length of the hindquarters be in balance with the forequarters. The pelvis (hip bone) should slope backwards and downwards from the spine at an angle of 30 degrees. The femur (upper thigh bone) should form a right angle with the pelvis. The lower thigh bone (stifle) should set at an angle of 45 degrees to the vertical. The pelvis and femur should be approximately equal in length. The ratio of the length of the femur to the tibia-fibula to the hock should be approximately as 4 : 5 : 3. The length of the lower leg, from the ground to the hock joint, should be a little less than 30 per cent of the distance from the ground to the top of the hip bones. The lower leg should be vertical to the ground. The hips should be broad, in balance with shoulders and ribcage. Hind legs strong and muscular, with well developed second thighs, denoting power and activity, but not cumbersome, set parallel to each other and well apart, in balance with forelegs and body. Feet as in forequarters. Faults: (S) Lack of proportion in bone. Poor angulation at hip-bone. Narrow hip structure. Stifle too straight or over-angulated. Cow hocks. Bowed hindlegs. Splay feet. (M) Feet turned in or out. White nails.

Gait

The gait should be free, balanced and vigorous. When viewed from the side the dog should have good reach in the forequarters and good driving power in the hindquarters. The back should be level and firm, indicating good transmission from rear to front. When viewed from the front (coming toward) or from the rear (going away), at a moderate pace, the dog shall track in two parallel lines, neither too close together nor too far apart, so placed as to give a strong well-balanced movement. The toes (fore and hind) should point straight ahead.

Direction to Exhibitors and Judges

The dog should be moved in the ring at a sufficient speed to show fluidity of movement, and not at a slow walk. Faults: (S) Rolling, paddling, or weaving when gaited. Any crossing movement, either front or rear. Stilted and restricted movement. (Dogs with structural weakness as evidenced by poor movement should not be used for breeding.)

Disqualifications

Liver mask. No mask. Yellow eyes.

3

Choosing a Puppy

Having decided on a Bullmastiff, don't be so impatient that you buy the first puppy you see advertised in your local newspaper. Also make sure that you do not fall for the salesmanship tricks in commercial kennels, where hundreds of puppies of every colour and shape can be viewed in their glass-fronted pens – on seeing them many people will quite often buy one for all the wrong reasons. As the old saying goes, 'Act in haste and repent at leisure', and it is appropriate here for buying a puppy on impulse will inevitably lead to heartache later on.

The dangers of buying a puppy through a free advertisment placed in the press by a so-called breeder are many and varied. If a breeder is unduly concerned about paying for an advert, then it gives cause for concern as to how the puppies have been reared. Many buyers have fallen prey to 'backyard breeders', by which we mean anyone who buys a bitch, usually the cheapest he can get regardless of quality, and who then proceeds to breed from her, often mating her to any dog he can obtain the service of cheaply. There is no guarantee that the resulting puppies are legally registered with The

Young hopefuls.

Kennel Club, or that the fancy pedigree certificate is authentic. Once you buy such a puppy you are stuck with him and will probably never see the breeder again. The cash you handed over will have gone for ever, and usually your dreams of showing and possibly breeding from your new dog will have gone with it.

Most people generally have no idea whom they should contact once they have decided to buy a Bullmastiff puppy. Our advice is and always has been that you should go to the library and read as much as you can about the breed. Also check out the two canine weekly magazines that can be obtained through your local newsagent, namely *Dog World* and *Our Dogs*. These magazines give details about every dog show imaginable that is held in the UK, and much else besides.

The second point of contact, after you have researched the breed and are sure that this is the one for you, should be The Kennel Club (*see* Useful Addresses). Obtain from the Club the name and address of your local Bullmastiff club's secretary, who in turn will be able to supply you with information as to when and where the club's shows will be held.

Once you are aware of the dates and venues of future club shows, the next step is to attend a few, where you will have the opportunity of examining the breed at close quarters and meeting breeders and exhibitors. If you are then still sure this is to be your chosen breed you will need to establish whether a Bullmastiff will fit in with your way of life, and whether you are going to fit in with his. Talk to people and ask as many questions as you can think of, for you need to know a lot about an animal that is going to live with you for the next ten or twelve years. Look, listen, and learn.

When you have finally decided on the kennel that produces the type of stock you like, you must contact that particular breeder and make an appointment to go and discuss your requirements in more detail. Be honest with the breeder and admit that you know very little, if anything, about the breed. Don't be afraid or nervous to discuss what you think you need or want to know – remember that it is you who wishes to buy the puppy. Also let the breeder know from the start whether you want a puppy with prospects for showing and possibly breeding, or just purely and simply a pet that will keep you company. Most reputable breeders will be only too pleased to help and advise you, and to answer your questions no matter how trivial you think they may be. The main wish of all such breeders is to see that their puppies are placed in caring, loving, and responsible homes. They are generally very particular about whom they sell their puppies to and are more than happy when you show genuine interest in the breed.

There is a vast difference between show-quality and pet puppies, especially in terms of price. It would be dishonest to inform a breeder that you only require a puppy of pet quality, to purchase him at a much reduced price, and then later to show and eventually breed from him. If a breeder sells a puppy of pet quality it is because he does not consider the puppy to be of sufficient quality to either show or breed from, and you must always respect his opinion in these matters. If you require a show-quality puppy, then make this clear at the very beginning.

A reputable breeder will do all in his power to help you choose a promising puppy. It is our advice that first and foremost you purchse a well-bred top-quality bitch puppy, if possible from line-bred parents, having first looked at her sire, her dam, and her brothers and sisters. Try to purchase a bitch puppy that is a good representative of the breed and that displays as few faults as possible. The breeder will guide you every inch of the way with regards showing, training, breeding, and so on. You may choose to purchase a well-bred, beautifully reared puppy which has taken the breeder many hard working years to develop. With such a puppy and the help and advice of his or her breeder you should be able to benefit and progress even further in your endeavour to establish your own breeding line.

Finally, do not buy cheap and expect a world-beater, for you will only get what you pay for. Also remember that there are no guarantees when you buy an animal – the most promising puppy may go wrong while a really ugly duckling can emerge into a beautiful swan. It is only with the help of an experienced breeder that you may be able to avoid some of the pitfalls, and believe us there will be lots of them on the way.

What to Look For

First and foremost you should be looking for a fit, healthy puppy; that is to say one that feels firm to the touch but does not carry excess fat, and is not so thin that you can see parts of his skeleton. Some of the basic signs of good health are bright eyes, a cool, moist nose, playfulness, soundness in limb, a coat in good condition, and a wagging tail.

Before you even look at individual puppies in a litter it is essential that you check the conditions in which they are being kept. A clean environment not only helps to keep the puppies sweet-smelling and happy, but also discourages the parasites that cause most skin problems. The puppies should be kept in clean, dry conditions with bedding such as pine shavings and sleeping quarters that consist of a large plastic bed and washable blanket.

Resign yourself before you begin the selection process to allocating plenty of time to choose your puppy. Remember that the puppy you choose will be your companion for the next decade, so you must be compatible. First impressions are lasting ones, and are very important if you are to be completely satisfied. Try to put colour preferences to the back of your mind so that they do not influence your final decision; type and compatibility should come first, then colour, for it would be unwise to overlook a superior puppy just because his colouring was not your preferred choice. Always try to take your pick from a whole litter, bearing in mind that the breeder will usually have already selected one for himself. The breeder cannot keep all of the puppies, so you should be able to obtain a quality, well-bred dog that has just as much promise as the breeder's own choice.

Next, look at the condition of the puppies. Dull, cloudy eyes could be a sign of general ill health. Running or weepy eyes could be attributed to entropion, ectropion, blocked tear ducts, ulcers on the lens, conjunctivitis, respiratory disease, or simply physical damage to the eye. The eyes should always be clear. The white of the eye must be a clear white with no red or any other signs of inflammation. A dry, cracked, warm nose could be indicative of a high temperature, or of a dog that is generally run down. A discharging nose could be symptomatic of many illnesses and should always be viewed with caution.

Puppies should be playful and quite happy to romp around; puppies that lie in a huddle may be doing so because they have intestinal problems or find it painful to play about. If a puppy's coat is in poor condition it may have intestinal worms, a poor diet, or general subclinical ill health. Patches of bare skin or old scabs in some cases denote mange or dermatitis, usually associated with dirty living conditions and a poor environment.

Where possible see at least three or four puppies from the same litter as this should give you an idea of the general health of the litter. All puppies should be happy, mischievous, active, and playful. When you have three or four to choose from let them run free as you

Ch. Graecia Celestine (by Ch. Danny Boy, out of Ch. Celeste of Graecia).

may find in doing so that one appeals to you more than the others – a great deal can be gleaned from watching a litter at play.

With regards to temperament, you certainly don't want a puppy that is either timid, nervous, or vicious, as such a puppy isn't displaying the true character of the Bullmastiff. Be wary of any puppy that hides in the kennel or shies away from you; natural wariness is acceptable but care must be taken that it is not a symptom of nervousness or unreliability, which should not be encouraged in the Bullmastiff. Only make your choice from those puppies that are friendly and outgoing. Any animal that shows viciousness, fear or hysterical behaviour should be avoided at all costs as such tendencies could take years to breed out of a line, if at all. As these behavioural problems have a nasty habit of recurring generations down the line when you least expect them, and as any dog displaying these traits can only damage the reputation of the breed, we would strongly recommend that you do not keep such a dog.

As the puppies are running free you should observe their basic limb movements to the full. All you need to do when assessing a puppy at this stage is to make sure that his legs move parallel to one another as he comes towards you and heads away again. While the puppies are playing you would be well advised to look for free and

Ch. Leyrigg French Pickle of Meitza.

easy movement with no undesirable traits such as limping, dragging the feet, or stilted or restricted movement. When in action the puppy should hold his head erect, proud and alert.

Some of the puppies will be more curious about you, so when they come close to you take the opportunity to lift them up and examine them in detail. Turn the puppy over onto his back and examine the belly, groin, and armpits, questioning any abrasions, rawness, or discoloration you may see. Pay particular attention to the genitals: a male puppy must have two testicles descended normally into the scrotum, and although it is not unusual to find one testicle a little higher than the other it must be easily found on examination. And while it is difficult to see both testicles in a small puppy it should not be too difficult to feel them. A cryptorchid dog (with only one testicle descended) or a bilateral cryptorchid (with neither testicle descended) is of little value to anyone who is contemplating breeding or showing. The puppy's navel should be neat and should be examined for any sign of a hernia; umbilical hernias, unless large, should not present a problem.

Even in a puppy that is only eight weeks old it is possible to discern the physical properties he will display at adulthood. The head should be large and square, although at this age a slight domed effect is acceptable. There should be plenty of width between the eyes, the colour of which must be as dark as possible. All puppies' eyes shortly after birth are blue, and the darker the shade of blue at this stage the darker will be the colour of the eyes in adulthood.

The ears at this age should be of small to medium size, remembering that the ratio of ear size to head size is slightly less in the adult dog. They should, of course, be darker than the body colour. Ear shape and carriage are not easy to predict as they often change several times during teething, and it is wise therefore to wait until teething is finished before trying to help them fold in the correct position. On the other hand, size and placement of the ears are hereditary, so it is a good idea to see your chosen puppy's parents if you need any guidance in this area.

With regards to the mouth, one that is slightly overshot or that has a scissor bite in a puppy eight to ten weeks old will on most occasions finish level or just a little undershot. Likewise, an undershot mouth at this age will tend to finish more undershot in adulthood. The underjaw should be broad and the teeth regular and well placed. The muzzle should not be too long at this age, as the ratio of length of muzzle to length of head increases in adulthood. The muzzle must be black and there should be black rings around the eyes that do not extend beyond them. We have found it very unlikely that the pigment of the muzzle either deepens or expands, but rather have found that the opposite is more common so that it lightens in colour and shrinks in area.

Moving on to the body, the back from shoulders to tail should be short and level, although at eight to ten weeks a slight rise over the loin is acceptable. Even in a puppy so young one should be able to ascertain a reasonable spring of rib, and the ribcage should be well extended backwards to give good length, together with a good depth. Take this opportunity to feel for the sternum, which should be well forward of the front legs even at this age.

The puppy should show well-developed hindquarters with good angulation. View with suspicion any degree of bandiness or cowhocks as these conditions do not always correct themselves; again, ask the breeder for his advice with regards to the parents at a similar age. Examine the tail from top to bottom: it should be smooth with no

Christmas spirit.

hint of a crank tail (it has been indicated that this trait may have been inherited from the old bulldog).

As you near the end of your detailed examination of the puppy's physical qualities, remember to check the feet and the pasterns. The feet should be well formed, with little or no signs of splaying, and the pasterns should be firm; if this is not the case the puppy may be either too fat or heavy, may not have had the opportunity of free play and exercise, or may have been fed a diet that is deficient in the required vitamins and minerals.

Next check the pigmentation. The nose should be black, as should the muzzle and the ring around the eyes. The toenails should be dark and the ears darker than the body colour. Avoid a puppy that has too much white on his chest; while it is acceptable to have a very small white mark on the chest this is undesirable, and there should certainly be no other white anywhere else on the animal. Although a coat of a clear colour is stipulated, it is quite acceptable for puppies to display a darker caste of black hairs. In the vast majority of cases this will diminish over the first few months of a puppy's life and reveal the true colour of the coat. A brindle should show well-defined brindling and should not have large patches of black. Care must be taken to check for the mask in a brindle, as it is sometimes difficult to define (we have seen many brindles that on close examination were found to have no mask). A good rule of thumb is that the colour shown on the top of the head of a very young puppy of eight weeks or so is quite often the final colour of the adult.

With regards to size, it is not always the largest puppy in the litter that finishes as the largest adult. Indeed, such a dog may even develop into a coarse Bullmastiff. The most important factor in a working breed is balance: everything about the puppy must be square.

By now you will have spent a great deal of time with the puppies and their breeder. If you wish to breed from your puppy in the future you must discuss the dam with the breeder before you make your final choice. Remember that family traits tend to pass from one generation to the next, so ask whether the dam whelped easily and if she was a good mother to her puppies. Finally, if you are in any doubt about a particular aspect of the puppy don't forget to ask if it would be possible to see both the parents and any earlier siblings or other family members.

Paperwork

All reputable breeders will, at the time you purchase your puppy, usually furnish you with a folder containing the puppy's pedigree, The Kennel Club registration certificate signed and completed for the transfer of ownership, and an easy-to-follow diet sheet explaining what to feed, the amounts and frequency of feeds, and information on how these will vary as the puppy grows. Depending on the age of the puppy at the time of sale a vaccination certificate should also be included. If, as may be the case, the registration certificate has not yet been received from The Kennel Club, it is a wise precaution for the prospective owner to enquire whether or not the breeder has placed any endorsements on the registration, and if so what they are. The Kennel Club and some of the more well-known insurance companies can arrange insurance for a puppy, and you are well advised to take advantage of this.

4

Puppy Management

When you arrive home with the new nine- or ten-week-old puppy of your choice your house rules will have to change dramatically. No longer will you be able to leave shoes or other such chewable items lying around, for to your puppy your home is a big-game country in which everything has to be defeated and then taken to his bed for further inspection.

Settling In

One of the first major decisions you will have to make is whether you want your puppy to live in the house or outside in a kennel with a run. If he is to live in the house then you must first decide the location for his bed. The majority of households seem to favour the kitchen or utility room, with the bed in a quiet corner out of harm's way where the puppy can still keep a watchful eye on his new family. It is an advantage if the bed can be placed close to a door so that the puppy has easy access to the garden, thereby facilitating house-training.

After you arrive home with your puppy you may find he is not yet interested in eating the food the breeder has supplied. Don't worry, but instead allow him plenty of time to settle into his new home. It is quite possible that the puppy will be excited and want to explore his new surroundings, play with his new toys and family members, or just sleep.

An excellent way of settling your new puppy in on his first night in your home is to leave a radio on with the volume turned down very low; this way he can hear voices or music and will not feel too lonely. A large soft toy or similar will make an ideal bed companion and help to replace his absent litter-mates. If possible, it is a good idea to leave a blanket with the breeder a week before you collect your puppy so that he can place it in with the litter for a short time.

The blanket will then take on the scent of the puppy's dam and the rest of the litter, so that when it is moved to his new bed in your home the puppy will not feel quite so isolated and should be happy and contented.

If the puppy insists on crying at night, don't make the mistake of going to him and making a fuss over him, or, worse still, playing with him. Instead, reprimand him gently using only the tone of your voice. If this has no effect and the puppy continues to yell then it may be an idea to try an adaptation of the mother's behaviour in such a situation. While the mother will grab a puppy by the back of the neck and shake him, we suggest that you pick him up by the back of his neck, supporting him with your other hand. At the same time you must raise your voice and say 'No' to let the puppy know that this is unacceptable behaviour. Don't expect miracles immediately as the chances are you may have to repeat the procedure several times before the puppy gets the message.

Beds and Bedding

We have found that the best type of bed is a large, oval, plastic one, preferably with a metal rim, similar to those used by the police force and armed services for their dogs. This type of bed is both tough and durable, and is also extremely easy to keep clean. Simply wash the bed with warm, soapy water and then wipe it over with a cloth moistened with an antiseptic solution. It will dry in a very short space of time.

You can then place into the bed a blanket or, preferably, a large piece of Vetbed bedding (this is an artificial fleece that allows any moisture to sink through to the bottom layer so that the top remains dry). A second very good form of bedding is a polystyrene beanbag, which can be used in conjunction with a plastic bed or as a separate bed providing it is covered with a strong material and is well filled. The beanbag cover should be made from a hard-wearing fabric such as denim, and should also be removable so that it can be washed and dried separately from the inner bag that contains the beans. If at any time the inner bag needs to be washed it can either be opened and the beans removed prior to washing, or it can be washed as a complete item as the polystyrene beans will not absorb moisture. Do not, however, use heat for drying the whole bag as the beans will melt; instead just hang it on the line to drip-dry.

From the very earliest stage you must teach your puppy that his bed is his own place. It will then become his retreat and refuge, and, if he is anything like some of our puppies, he will take everything into it. Remember also that you made it his place and so you must respect it as such.

Kennels

Sometimes it is more convenient to house a puppy outdoors in a kennel and run. We find that most owners who do this tend to use a kennel whenever they have to leave their puppy unattended.

While it may not always be possible to situate a kennel ideally, perhaps due to space restrictions, try to place it so that it faces south or south-east. The main reasons for this is that during the day in winter the puppy will benefit from any available sunlight, and also that cold northerly winds will not be able to blow into the kennel entrance. The latter particularly applies in more northerly areas of the northern hemisphere.

There are numerous designs of dog kennel available, but whichever you choose it must be constructed from strong materials, and must be warm and draught-free in the winter and cool in the hot summer months. If you choose a wooden kennel it is advantageous

Ch. Verona of Oldwell.

to fit insulation material with a thickness of approximately 2½in (6cm) between the outer and inner walls. If it is built of brick, and unless it has cavity walls, then the walls should be thick enough to compensate for the lack of insulation materials. Ideally the kennel should be raised off the ground by some 6in (15cm). This will enable all water underneath to run away and will allow a free flow of air under the floor, thereby eliminating the contributory causes of damp. The space underneath will also make cleaning easier.

The inside of the kennel should be divided and constructed in such a way as to allow the puppy access to a sleeping area, which must be raised at least 4in (10cm) above the floor and protected from all draughts. Whatever the design of kennel it must have ample ventilation and, in some cases, some form of heating. Over many years we have used infrared lamps, which we have found to be excellent. If you do use such a lamp you must position it over one end of the bed only so that your puppy has space to move away from it if necessary. The internal area of the kennel must also be large enough to allow the puppy space to play during inclement weather conditions.

With regards to bedding, you can use either a plastic bed or a beanbag as mentioned earlier, along with pine-wood shavings or shredded paper; all these can easily be kept clean, either by washing in the case of the bed and beanbag or sterilizing in the case of the shavings and paper. The disadvantages of using straw and hay are that they may introduce mites or fleas into your kennel.

The puppy should also have access to an exercise area that ideally should be easy to clean and disinfect. To contain the puppy a fence can be constructed from panels that are obtainable ready made for the purpose. Failing this, a simple pen can be made using a wooden frame onto which chain-link fencing or Weldmesh is secured. Weldmesh is the trade name for a type of fencing material that is constructed from lengths of wire of various thickness welded together to form a panel of small squares, thereby making it similar in appearance to a net.

See Chapter 5 for information on adult kennelling.

Feeding

Feeding is the next important regime to organize. It is to be hoped that you will have received a diet sheet from the puppy's breeder informing you how the puppy has been reared from weaning until

SA Ch. Chizlehurst Chief of Rainel, pictured here at seventeen months.

the time you collect him. This should detail the various foods and amounts used in the diet, along with vitamin supplements, and should also include the times and frequency of feeds. Finally, it should give guidance as to what future quantities will be required to maintain both optimum growth rate and development.

Never be tempted to change a puppy's diet at this most important time in the belief that you know more about him than his breeder does or because the puppy's food does not seem apetizing to you. If you do so you may be making one of the worst decisions of your puppy's life: sickness and diarrhoea, plus appalling intestinal upsets, are but a short step away. Veterinary surgeons will tell you that they see innumerable puppies each year with severe intestinal and digestive problems that have been caused entirely by incorrect feeding.

From the time when your puppy was weaned from his mother the breeder will have fed him good wholesome food, either in the form of a proprietary prepared puppy food or a more natural diet. There are on the market many and varied commercially produced foods that are specially formulated for young puppies. According to the manufacturers they contain all the vitamins, minerals, trace elements, and nutrients a young puppy should ever need. On the other hand, many breeders of long standing will have developed their own tried and tested feeding programme using various natural commodities.

Many people who acquire a puppy – especially if he is the first dog they have owned – fail to realize that he needs proportionately far more high-quality food than an adult. In fact, a puppy will possibly need more than double the amount per unit of body weight than an adult just to keep pace with his rapid growth and development. Contrary to popular belief, it is our opinion that puppies only require a diet with 20–25 per cent protein content at the time of weaning, although this should increase to the upper limit shortly after weaning. Avoid feeding extra-high levels of protein as this can force growth and may contribute to various skeletal problems.

If you are feeding a meat-based diet (with, of course, a good-quality wholemeal biscuit and all other necessary foods), as many types of meat as possible should be included. Only meat that has been passed as fit for human consumption should be considered fit for your puppy. All meats are high in phosphorus and low in calcium, so if you feed only meat to a puppy to such an extent that his appetite is fully satisfied you may be storing up trouble for the future. The correct ratio of phosphorous to calcium should be as 1:1.2 in order to facilitate the correct absorption of calcium. It is essential that meats included in the diet should not consist solely of lean muscle, but also all types of offal and a minimum of 5 per cent fat as these contain the various nutrients necessary for a puppy's healthy development. However, never feed offal to excess as it may result in a vitamin imbalance or even, in extreme cases, vitamin poisoning (hypervitaminosis).

We recommend that you feed protein from as many different sources as possible, including meat, eggs, milk, yeast, fish, and cheese. However, only feed small amounts of the latter as dogs cannot digest all cheeses, and also be aware of the fact that some puppies may have a lactose intolerance, which can cause severe diarrhoea.

Olympia Colossus, bred by Alfred and Beatrice Adaikalaraj of Malaysia, at only seven months!

We believe that protein from animal sources is far more advantageous to a dog than that from vegetable or cereal sources as it is better absorbed and therefore utilized by the dog.

While it is true that many years ago dogs were reared with far different feeding regimes from this modern approach, it must be noted that as dogs are now shorter and heavier in build their skeleton has to support a greater burden. The present-day dog also reaches his full growth potential much sooner, and hence more strain is put on skeletal formation. For these reasons modern breeds of heavily built dogs will also require mineral supplements to be added to their everyday diets.

Your new puppy may not be all that concerned about eating when he first arrives in your home. Now that he is away from his littermates the stimulation and competition that takes place at mealtimes will no longer exist. However, don't panic as he will eat when he is good and ready. Whatever you do, don't start offering titbits in the hope that you will persuade him to eat, but instead leave him until he is really hungry – usually only a matter of a few hours after arrival. Providing a bowl of clean water is available at all times the puppy will come to no harm from such an approach and will eagerly relish

Poachersfoe Prospector (by Ch. Graecia Mercury, out of Ch. Dajean Golddust the Poachers foe), aged six and a half months.

his next meal without looking up from his feeding bowl. Once again, we must stress that it is essential that you stick to the breeder's feeding regime and always take notice of what he advises in terms of feeding and diet.

See Chapter 5 for information on adult diets.

Worming

Ask the breeder when the puppy was last wormed and which preparation was used. Also ascertain how often the puppy has already been wormed and when this procedure will need to be repeated. Depending on the preparation, it is advisable to administer worming pills from an early age and on a regular basis. We usually begin when the puppy is about four weeks of age and continue until he is approximately four months old, repeating the treatment every two or three weeks. From then until the dog is twelve months old we worm approximately every three months. While the exact time intervals are not too important, the puppy must be wormed at least three times between the ages of four and twelve months.

81

When a puppy defecates after he has been wormed he will also expel large numbers of worm eggs, and these will need to be destroyed to ensure that they cannot develop into infective larvae. The safest way to deal with these is to clean up immediately and, if at all possible, to use a blowlamp to scorch the affected area.

There are various preparations available on the market to deal with the worms; some are administered to eliminate a single type of worm while others may be of a compound composition designed to deal with several types. We recommend the following:

1. Piperazine citrate, a relatively old but well-tried and tested drug with an excellent success rate, used particularly to treat roundworm infestation.
2. Pyrantel-Pamoates, suitable for treating hookworm.
3. Bendazoles, and in particular Fenbendazole, an excellent all-round worming preparation. It is usually administered over a three-day period and is particularly effective when a heavy infestation is suspected.
4. Drontal-Plus, an excellent all-round wormer which is gentle yet effective against most types of worms. As far as we are aware it has very few, if any, side-effects.

Inoculations

By the time you get your puppy it is possible his inoculation programme has already commenced (reputable breeders usually start inoculations for any puppies over the age of ten weeks that are still with them). If this is the case take the puppy's record card (which you will have received when you collected the puppy) to the veterinary surgeon of your choice. He should then be able to advise you as to which inoculations are still required for the course to be complete, and at what ages they should be given.

Inoculations are usually administered on two separate visits, with varying intervals between each dose depending on the age of the puppy and the vaccines used. They should protect your puppy against distemper, hardpad, parvovirus, leptospirosis (both canicola and icterhaemorrgia), hepatitis, and parainfluenza (commonly referred to as kennel cough). Unfortunately, not all strains of kennel cough can be vaccinated against, although there is a nasal vaccine that helps protect against most of the viruses (see Chapter 10).

Ch. Tartuffe Priam.

Daily Routine

Organize your own and the puppy's schedule right from the very first morning as it will pay dividends over and over again if you start as you mean to go on by setting a routine and sticking to it. Greet your puppy with a warm, friendly gesture each morning; let him know you are happy to see him. Give your puppy the opportunity to relieve himself as soon as you can – remember that it will have been a long night for such a little puppy – and whilst he is doing so you can prepare his breakfast. After he has eaten allow him to relieve himself again, and the same applies after he wakes from a nap or has been playing.

Always let the puppy go out into the garden to relieve himself after every meal regardless of all other considerations, and when he has done so make a fuss and praise him. Never punish your puppy when he has an accident, as he undoubtedly will. Try to remember that it is not entirely the puppy's fault, and that it is as much your fault as you were not quick enough to realize that he needed to relieve himself. Instead, pick the puppy up and let him know, using

83

only the tone of your voice, that this is not allowed, then take him outside immediately and show him where you wish him to relieve himself. Pay particular attention to the puppy's signals, as he will soon become frustrated if you cannot understand the signs.

If your puppy has previously been accustomed to relieving himself on newspaper (as is the common practice with a number of breeders), then continue to use this method to begin with. Slowly, over a period of a few days, move the paper closer to the door to your garden, eventually placing a couple of sheets of newspaper actually in the garden. If the weather is warm enough, you could also feed your puppy outdoors in the garden. If possible, follow this routine for all meals and make many more trips into the garden throughout the day. Within a very short space of time your puppy will learn the correct place to relieve himself so that accidents in the house become less and less frequent. The most important point to remember here is that a puppy learns by repetition; if you continually praise your puppy when he gets it right then it should take only a short period of time before he is completely house-trained. This should encourage the puppy to use the desired place.

Don't forget that you have to cater to the puppy's every need at this age. Not only will he need feeding every four hours or so, but he will also need something to keep him occupied for the short times you are not with him. Large plastic mineral-water bottles, with the screwtops removed, make cheap and ideal toys. As they are light and durable they will keep a puppy actively interested for hours on end.

When you are at home with the puppy you will need to teach him how to behave around the house: no chewing the furniture, articles of footwear, and the like, and no grabbing electrical or telephone wires in his mouth. To prevent the destruction of shoes by chewing, always pick them up off the floor and keep them out of harm's way, for if the puppy cannot get at them he cannot then be blamed for chewing them. The same goes for children's toys – remove all temptation and give the puppy his own toys or a large knucklebone to play with. While cats or adult dogs in the house will soon learn to keep out of the puppy's way, never allow the puppy to take liberties with older animals. There are many tolerant dogs which will be quite happy to play with a young puppy, but others may cause a defenceless puppy a great deal of irreparable damage, so please take care. Also take care if you have children, for a puppy will be entirely at their mercy. Puppies will bite their litter-mates during play, so to avoid them behaving in the same natural way with children it is

Ch. Bournvalley Oakenargen at Meitza.

important to give the puppy something to play with of his own and to teach the children to respect him.

Training

When your puppy has finished his inoculations and adequate time has elapsed to allow the vaccine to give full protection, he can be taken out on a collar and lead. Some puppies take to the collar and lead like ducks to water, whilst others look and act as though they were taking part in a rodeo. Allow him to wear a soft puppy collar all the time at first, as in this way he will get used to it after a very short time and ignore it completely. An old, short lead can then be attached to this collar and the puppy can drag it around the house for short periods until he is accustomed to it.

The next step is to take hold of the end of the lead and to let the puppy take you for a walk; don't pull back on the lead at this stage as the puppy may panic when he feels the restraint around his neck. If the puppy is quite happy with you on the other end of the lead then encourage him to come to you instead. Little by little, the puppy will get the message, especially if you reward him with a small treat each time he comes to your call. Eventually, the puppy will be happy to follow you whilst on a lead. It is only then, when the puppy knows what is required of him, that you should venture out to walk him on his lead.

When the time comes to go for the first walk, remember that the puppy is still only a baby and will soon tire if you walk him further than he is capable of. He will be happy and curious, wanting to investigate all the new sights, but it is imperative that you recognize any signs of tiredness immediately, such as rolling the head from side to side, stopping and rolling over, or sitting and panting. Do not get carried away with the fact that your puppy seems to be enjoying himself, and definitely do not be tempted to walk so far that you have to carry him home – such a long walk may seriously damage your puppy.

Once the puppy has got used to the lead you should teach him to walk correctly on it as a dog that pulls can be tiresome and a downright nuisance, as well as being dangerous. A Bullmastiff puppy grows very quickly, and the last thing you want is for something that grows almost to the size of a young lion cub to pull you off your feet or, worse still, into the path of traffic. Start as you mean to go on, and don't allow him to pull you anywhere at any time. If the puppy should start to pull then a sharp tug on the lead combined with the command 'Heel' will, in time, bring him under control. A further way to combat pulling is to do an about turn and proceed to walk in the opposite direction as soon as the puppy begins to pull.

After a few of these lessons you should find yourself with a dog you can be proud of. Never, under any circumstances, let your puppy get out of hand, and let him know that you disapprove of unacceptable behaviour. If you ask the puppy to do something, make sure he does, even if it takes all day for him to do so. If the puppy learns by experience that he can ignore you then he will always take advantage of this.

Once your puppy has mastered house- and lead-training, you can introduce new adventures. If you intend to show your puppy you will need to find out about ringcraft clubs (not to be confused with obedience training clubs) in your area. These will usually be advertised in your local library or veterinary surgery; further sources of information include the canine press – namely *Our Dogs* and *Dog World* magazines – and The Kennel Club.

At ringcraft you and your puppy will be taught the basic rudiments required in the show ring. Your puppy is taught to stand correctly and at the same time to allow someone to examine him, just as would happen in the show ring when he is being checked by a judge. Although ringcraft clubs are usually run on a weekly basis, a great deal more can be done in the confines of your own home. The biggest benefit your puppy will get from such a class is socializing with people and other dogs. This socialization should continue on your shopping trips, when you collect the children from school, and when friends and family visit.

5

Adolescent and Adult Management

The Adolescent

From the age of approximately four months you will notice that the shape of your puppy changes to that of an adolescent, with longer legs and a rangier body. At this stage the level topline he may once have had is now anything but level, and the rear end seems to belong to a different dog than that of the front, making him appear to have much shorter front legs. This is all part of growing up, and in time he will change again. While the adolescent dog is with you the name of the game is patience, for with luck your ugly duckling will emerge into a beautiful swan.

Lin Toosey, owned by Mr and Mrs W. Scott.

Adolescent dogs seem at times to almost grow by the hour, so that by the time they are ten or twelve months old they should have attained their full adult height. Despite this, adolescents are still very immature in physical terms – just as a teenage boy differs greatly from his father. The rate at which dogs mature varies – whereas some lines mature very quickly, others seem to take for ever. A youngster from one line could, by the time he is twelve months old, look and act like a fully grown adult, while a youngster of similar age bred from another line could still be very much a puppy at the same age. We have noticed over the years that dogs that reach maturity early also, in the majority of cases, show signs of old age earlier. It has even been known for some of these dogs to die of old age before they have reached their seventh year.

We believe in letting our dogs remain youngsters for as long as possible so that they enjoy their youth to the full. They do appear to take a long time to mature – usually three years or more – but we are rewarded by the fact that they take their time. In general, they lead an active life until old age starts to creep up on them at about nine years. They then begrudgingly begin to slow down, but they still always go through a second childhood whenever puppies or younger dogs appear on the scene.

During this formative time in a dog's life make sure you devote all the time, love, and attention you can to him. This is the time when you will form a bond that lasts for life.

Training

For their own safety and yours, basic obedience should be taught to all dogs, whatever their breed, preferably while they are still young. Like all teenagers the adolescent dog needs gentle but firm handling. Adolescence is a time to re-enforce the early lessons of puppyhood, and to build on these lessons. For example, your puppy will have been taught how to walk correctly on a lead and to behave with good manners. The next stage – undertaken in adolescence – is to encourage him to walk to heel. This can be done by gently bringing his head level with your leg and at the same time giving him the command 'Heel'. Once he has mastered this you should begin to walk with the dog and at the same time give him the command. If your youngster is like some of ours have been, he will more than likely get so close to your leg that he will trip you up! With repetition, however, it will only take a short time before he becomes used to the idea. If you own a youngster who finds it hard to learn to walk to heel, you will soon find success with the help of a head collar.

With a dog that consistently insists on jumping up to greet people, you should get into the habit each time he does so of pushing your knee into his chest, and at the same time giving the command 'Down'. If he is already on a lead, then give it a sharp tug and again give the command. Eventually he will get the message. All dogs should be taught at this early age to respect their owners and other people. The last thing you want when friends come to visit is for the young dog to jump up at them. A youngster should also be taught to respect and accept all other animals. This will obviously make life much easier for you in the future if you intend to show him. We have actually seen a dog rear up on his hindlegs, screaming to get at another in a ring – much to the embarrassment of his owner.

Jess, owned and trained by Mrs K. Lewis, competes in Agility.

Ch. Naukeen Liela.

Health

It is important at this stage to start grooming. The first things to take care of are the ears and teeth. During this formative time the young-ster should be taught to let people examine him in detail, especially if he is to be exhibited later. The Breed Standard specifies that Bullmastiff ears should fold in a V shape; because ears of this type are kept folded close to the head they may need regular checking and cleaning, and as such it is imperative the dog learns from an early age to stand still whilst you do so. The same goes for teeth and eyes – not only will you need to examine them closely, but future judges will also want to do so and will not like it if the dog is jumping about.

The next aspect that demands attention is the nails. If the dog gets plenty of exercise you should never have to clip his nails, but on the off chance you do it is as well to get him used to the idea whilst he is still a youngster. If you try to clip the nails of a fully grown dog who has never experienced this before, the chances are that you could end up on your back with him standing by laughing.

Like all youngsters, your dog will no doubt be bursting with energy. The best way to expend this energy, apart from allowing him to play with other dogs, is to take him out for walks. Ideally this should consist of a mixture of roadwork while under control on a lead, and running on grasslands and over rough, variable terrain off the lead – if possible, up hill and down dale. Obviously you should use your own common sense here with regards to the amount of exercise allowed at any one time. Start gradually and increase slowly to build muscle volume as the adolescent approaches adulthood.

Diet

Tremendous strides forward have been made over the years in the manufacture of different dog feeds. These have ranged from brown bread, stock cubes, offal, and, indeed, anything that owners could lay their hands on during the war years to the exotic feeds that are available today to all types of dogs. There are now also many types of feeding regimes, the most common of which are the professionally manufactured complete feeds, meat, tinned food and mixers, and home-cooked food.

The requirements for all of these are the same: namely, to make sure that the dog receives nourishing food that contains adequate supplies of protein, carbohydrates, fats, vitamins, and minerals. At the time of writing it would appear that there are two distinct schools of thought in the UK with regards which feeding regime is best. One is for the professionally manufactured complete feeds, while the other champions the old-fashioned methods using home-cooked foods based on a varied diet.

Complete Feeds

These range from low-quality, low-protein, low-priced varieties to those containing ultra-high levels of protein that are claimed by their manufacturers to be the best. Most complete feeds are usually of a baked, extruded, and expanded composition in the form of cubes, rings, or cylindrical shapes, or a flaked-type mixture. They are formulated to supply the specific required amounts and ratios of nutrients, vitamins, and minerals for each type of dog: for example, puppy, adolescent, adult, working or performance, breeding or veteran. In addition to the standard, 'maintenance' diet for adults, some manufacturers produce a low-calorie variety for dogs that are overweight, and a hypo-allergenic one for those that are allergic to specific ingredients. Some highly specialized feeds are also manufactured for convalescent or chronically sick dogs. Due to the fact that they contain antioxidants and very little moisture, they have a shelf life of several months if kept cool and dry.

Over the years we have tried several of these feeds, and have found that while some have produced excellent results others have proved catastrophic. If you wish to use one of the manufactured feeds, then find out all you can about it by reading books on canine nutrition (see Bibliography). Do not be misguided by the pressure-sell points on the label, and instead check on such things as digestibility, acceptability to the dog, and the source of protein content. Remember always that in most cases the manufacturer's prime concern is to show a profit on its investment. Having said this, some of the larger, more well-known manufacturers have spent a great deal of time and even more money conducting research into the nutritional requirements of the dog.

The main components in the majority of these feeds are cereals, protein (of either animal or vegetable origin), animal derivatives, bone-meal, fish-meal, soya bean or soya-bean oil, fat, and various supplements. You should be wary of complete feeds that contain high amounts of fibre as in general these tend to have a very low digestibility rate and resultant high volumes of waste matter. Also be aware that it is not unknown for some manufacturers to add oils or fat to the finished product, as not only does this add the required amount of this component to the feed but it also makes the meal more palatable.

If you are using a complete feed, remember that it is not only unnecessary but can actually be counterproductive and downright dangerous to add vitamin supplements or other foods to it. After all the research that has been conducted on behalf of the manufacturer by qualified scientists and veterinary surgeons, all of whom have expert knowledge in the field of canine nutrition, it would seem pointless for an amateur to interfere with the balance of the product. Complete feeds are not only convenient to use, but as the name suggests they contain all the nutrients the dog should need. There is, however, no reason why different brands of complete feeds that have a similar nutritional content cannot be mixed or fed together to allow the dog variety in his feed.

Complete feeds can be fed either dry with drinking water made available, or they can be soaked in water or gravy. It is of paramount importance that fresh drinking water is available for the dog at all times when using these feeds.

If you are rearing a puppy on a complete feed don't forget to change to the appropriate feed as he grows. By the same rule, a working dog taking large amounts of exercise needs to be fed a meal that contains a higher protein and carbohydrate level than the basic maintenance diet, while an elderly dog needs a different type again.

The advantages of complete feeds are that they are extremely convenient, clean, and easy to use and store. If you are feeding a good-quality brand then the dog should need nothing other than water. The better-quality manufactured varieties have a great deal to recommend them, and when you consider the time, money, and effort that goes into making the finished product their benefits far outweigh any disadvantages.

The disadvantages are that their palatability does not suit all dogs. Some appear to be manufactured with cost and profit as prime considerations, and in our opinion the flake types of feeds appear to be a strange diet for a dog. In our experience some of the complete feeds also lead to greatly increased stool quantities, perhaps because the majority of the protein content may be derived from vegetable or cereal matter. With this type of protein a large volume of feed is needed to supply the dog with the necessary amounts, as opposed to animal protein, which would be required in smaller quantities.

Tinned Food

Most tinned food these days can also be classed as a complete feed, although you would need to feed large numbers of tins in order to supply the dog with sufficient carbohydrate for his energy demands, thereby wasting large quantities of protein. The main ingredients of tinned feeds are meats, fish, meat or fish by-products, vegetable matter, and cereals, plus a vitamin supplement. With those tins that lack cereal content it is advisable to feed a good-quality wholemeal mixer in addition to supply the extra carbohydrates required.

The better-quality varieties are those that contain no cereal or carbohydrates (and are hence high in protein), while the cheaper types contain varying quantities of cereals, sometimes at levels far in excess of the meat or fish content. Because of their moist texture and meat or fish content, tinned foods are highly palatable and extremely digestible, all of which will encourage the dog to eat sufficient quantities of them.

Home-Cooked Food

Some years ago we believed like many before us that the warming broth from a stew made from meat, chicken, and vegetables, poured over either biscuits or wholemeal bread, was the ideal meal for both puppies and adults. In those days, biscuits and meal were manufactured and graded in four main sizes: puppy meal, which measured approximately $\frac{1}{16}$in (2mm) in diameter; terrier meal, up to $\frac{1}{2}$in (1cm) in diameter; hound meal, up to 1in (2cm) in diameter; and whole biscuits, 1–4in (3–10cm) in diameter.

We felt satisfied in the knowledge that our dogs were being given the best food available. We used to buy cheaply any meat left unsold at a local butcher on a Saturday evening – including whole chickens, steaks, pork, lamb, liver, and even beefburgers and sausages – and made the stew with the addition of barley, rice, oats, and vegetables. We would then divide this, pack it, and place the packs in the freezer, putting sufficient in each pack to feed the dogs for a day when combined with wholemeal bread. The only other addition we used was a multivitamin supplement. This was the staple diet of all our dogs for over ten years, until we were informed by a veterinary surgeon who specialized in canine nutrition that, due to the cooking process and the interaction between the various ingredients, a large proportion of the vitamins, minerals, and nutrients were being destroyed or made unavailable to the dog's digestive system. He said that if the ingredients had been fed raw and separately they would have been far more beneficial. However, it seemed to us that we were doing right for doing wrong, for all our dogs at the time looked and performed well.

Some years later we tried the so-called complete feeds with varying results. We fed a large number of complete feeds in the ensuing years, but have now returned to what we consider a successful regime of meat, wholemeal biscuits, fruit, and vegetables, together with a vitamin supplement when needed.

When you are fulfilling the dog's nutritional requirements through home-cooked foods it is essential that you ensure the diet you supply is properly balanced.

The Balanced Diet

The requirements of a varied, well-balanced diet are that it must supply the correct amounts and ratios of proteins, carbohydrates, fat, vitamins, minerals, and water relative to the size and activity levels of the dog. We cannot stress enough the importance of this simple statement. You must get the diet correct right from the start if you wish to guarantee that your dog's development and growth are normal, and that he has a long and healthy life.

There was once a very widely held, but mistaken, belief that dogs are carnivores rather than omnivores, and that they should therefore be fed a diet of meat, meat, and more meat, all of it muscle meat. It was not unusual for dogs to be fed large quantities of meat and very little of anything else, other than the scraps from the family table. People who believed this to be the correct diet always used to state that dogs in the wild eat the flesh of animals they kill, and never eat vegetables or cereals. However, they conveniently forgot that in the wild a dog will devour all of the carcass, including the stomach and intestinal contents (often vegetarian in origin) of their prey, plus the bones and all vital organs.

A dog fed on a meat-only diet will show a vast improvement in just about every aspect in the beginning due to the high intake of proteins. However, within a very short space of time – perhaps as little as six months – he will begin to lose condition and suffer a general decline in health.

While there are some vegetarian dog owners who fulfil their dogs' protein needs with rice, lentils, soya, cereals, vegetables, and fruit, the majority of us do rely on meat for protein. It is imperative here that as many types of meat as possible are used, including lamb, pork, and chicken besides beef, as well as eggs, fish, milk, and cheese. It is also necessary to include different types of offal – such as heart, liver, kidney, spleen, and lungs, all of which contain vitamins and minerals essential for the dog's well-being – together with tripe and a quantity of fat. The fat content should be approximately 5–10 per cent of the total diet, depending on the amounts of exercise or work the dog normally undertakes. We also believe that the benefits a dog receives from consuming bones far outweigh any disadvantages. However, ensure the bones are fed raw, and do not under any circumstances feed bones that have been cooked.

The dog's carbohydrate requirement can be obtained not only from biscuits but also from various other sources, mainly vegetables and fruits, all of which will benefit him. These should be processed so that the cellulose walls of the plant cells, which the dog is unable to digest, are broken down. This can be achieved by either steaming or by pulverizing in a food processor. Prepared in such a way fruits and vegetables begin to resemble the stomach contents of a herbivore without the enzymes that are present in the gut. Such enzymes are beneficial to a dog, and fermented vegetable matter obtained from the rumen of a cow is in fact more valuable to the dog than the flesh of the cow, not only for these enzymes but also for the B-complex vitamins and other food materials it contains that cannot be obtained by the dog elsewhere.

Wild dogs will eat the intestines of animals they kill for this reason, and following on from this owners of old would include unwashed tripe and small amounts of the contents of the rumen in their dogs' diets. At one time we collected tripe from abattoirs and went to great lengths to wash and clean them, only to be informed by a knowledgeable vet that by so doing we were in fact removing most, if not all, of the enzymes utilized by the dog.

There are two distinct schools of thought as to whether meat should be fed raw or cooked. Cooking meat helps to destroy the bacteria responsible for salmonella and botulism, as well as other undesirable elements such as toxins introduced by moulds and the eggs and larvae of parasites, and generally makes the meat much safer to eat. Arguments against cooking state that it can, especially if overdone, destroy protein, vitamins, and minerals, thereby reducing the nutritional value of the food.

Feeding uncooked food is obviously more natural for the dog, whose whole digestive system has been adapted to deal with raw foods. In the wild the dog's food is not only raw, but as it takes a couple of days to devour a large carcass it is anything but fresh. Such raw, rotten meat would contain not only bacteria but parasites and their eggs. So if you do decide to feed your dog raw foods, it is essential that any meats fed have been passed fit for human consumption.

Kennelling

When it is inconvenient to keep your dogs in the house the only solution is outside kennels. However, remember that if you have to kennel your dogs outside then they will obviously get less attention than if they were in the house with you. If they are not given some

Damascene Colonel Bogie of Rodekes.

form of extra stimulation kennel dogs soon get bored. It is therefore your responsibility to make certain that you go to them and make a fuss of them at every opportunity. They will readily appreciate any small gesture from you and will also greatly benefit from the companionship of being taken for walks.

Kennel designs are many and varied, ranging from simple kennels for one dog to the luxurious kennel ranges of the multi-dog owner. They may be designed and constructed by experts at great expense, or created by owners with minimal outlay using materials such as straw bales.

Without taking such extreme measures it is possible to buy or construct a very satisfactory kennel at no great expense. Ready-made wooden or prefabricated kennels, available either singly or as multi-kennel blocks, can be purchased to suit almost anyone's requirements and taste, but for the DIY enthusiast it is a fairly simple task to construct one yourself. The advantage of this is that you can design and build the kennel to suit your own requirements, taking into account all the considerations of space and position available. Finally, if you intend to keep a large number of dogs you should seriously consider buying or building an isolation kennel. There are bound to be occasions when it will be necessary to have one, if not for a sick dog then perhaps as a means of keeping a bitch that is in season away from the other dogs.

Kennel Construction

The prime consideration after weather- and draught-proofing is the size of the kennel required to house a full-grown Bullmastiff. The internal height of the kennel should be such that the dog can stand erect in it with his head well clear of the roof. For your own personal convenience it would be much better if the internal height was at least 6ft (1.8m) as this will allow easy access for cleaning.

The kennel should have at least one opening window, or alternatively a shutter that can be opened like a window; this will provide light and, most importantly, ventilation. There must be an air vent, preferably positioned in the wall opposite the window, to allow a free flow of air through the kennel. The ideal door is a stable door, in other words one that is split into two. This will allow you to access the interior while still keeping the dog confined or, with only the bottom half open, allow the dog free access while helping to conserve heat within.

The actual sleeping area should be raised at least 6in (15cm) above the floor and will benefit from having some form of protection from draughts. We place a board just inside the entrance to the kennel, positioned in such a way that it forms a draught-proof barrier between the sleeping area and the rest of the kennel. The sleeping area should also be constructed so that any boards and beds are easily removed for cleaning.

The inside of the kennel can be painted with a non-toxic paint to aid cleaning; this should also help to preserve the wood. To deter chewing, either affix metal strips to all prominent edges of wood or apply a non-poisonous preparation such as Bitter Apples to exposed wood.

The outer walls of the kennel should be treated with a good-quality wood preservative, applied at least annually and possibly more frequently. There are many preservatives suited to this job, but you must make certain that the one you choose is safe to use around pets. The roof should be covered with a weatherproof material such as best-quality mineral felt. Do not be tempted to use cheaper felt as such materials tend to be adversely affected by the sun. The first wet weather after the sunny period will then reveal all the cracks and defects.

It will benefit the dogs if you line and insulate the inside of the kennel. The insulation materials used should not be attractive to fleas or other undesirables. Solid sheets of polystyrene cut to size are excellent for this purpose, but consult your local building inspector or builder's merchant for advice on suitable materials. After the insulation materials have been fitted, then an inner skin, possibly of plywood, can be applied to cover the interior of the kennel.

Ideally, kennels should stand 6–8in (15–20cm) off the ground to allow all water to drain away and to allow air to flow freely. This will help to prevent the accumulation of damp under the kennel that might otherwise damage the structure.

The Run

The ground on which the kennel stands must be hard and firm enough to cope with the weight of both the dog and kennel combined. It should have a gradient of at least 1 in 40 to allow excess water to drain off quickly.

You need to choose between either a concrete or paving-slab base and prepare the ground accordingly. If a concrete base is to be used then the ground must be prepared with a firm bed of hardcore, onto which the cement can be laid. If you prefer to pave the area, then again you should have a firm base. The paving slabs should be laid on a 2in (5cm) bed of sharp sand and cement, mixed in rough proportions of five parts sand to one part cement and laid dry. It is most important if using paving slabs to ensure that the gaps between them are completely filled, otherwise they will soon accumulate urine and excrement, or water may run into them to damage the bed on which the stones are laid.

Over the years we have tried various different types and sizes of fencing around runs but have finally settled in favour of 6ft-high

Ewart Grant's Ch. Jagopeeko Wood Sorrell.

(1.8m) framed panels. These are made from a 1in square (6.5cm sq) box-section frame, onto which is welded a 2in square (13cm sq) wire mesh, all galvanized to prevent rust. The panels are completely interchangeable, and can readily be purchased from numerous suppliers. Some fence panels can also be bought with a ring attached to them, in which a dog's feeding bowl can be held.

The size of each pen will depend on the space available. Our pens are 8ft (2.4m) wide by 20ft (6m) long, the size we consider large enough to house a dog and bitch (we always keep our dogs in pairs as we believe they enjoy one another's company – you only have to watch them at play to realize this). In this size of pen each pair has a kennel 8ft (2.4m) wide by 4ft (1.2m) deep.

During the summer months we arrange shade netting over the kennels and runs to protect the dogs from the heat of the sun. It does not take very long for a dog to become overheated when sleeping in full sun, so such protection is beneficial. We also always leave a bench in each run for the dogs so that they don't have to lie on the hard floor (this can cause calluses and pressure sores, which once

101

formed are extremely difficult to put right). Such a bench can be made as a platform 40in square (250cm sq) in area and 6in (15cm) high, or you could use a tubular-frame bed over which either canvas or hessian has been stretched to form a hammock.

Bedding

You can choose from bedding used for dogs kept indoors (*see* Chapter 4) or from various other materials that are only suited to outdoor use. A very popular choice of kennel bedding with owners in the UK is straw. This has the obvious drawbacks of harbouring fleas, but on the plus side it is cheap, easily obtainable, and the dogs soon make a warm, cosy bed in it. Rye straw does not appear to be associated with fleas to the same extent as oat or barley straw.

There are few better bedding materials than wood wool. It is, however, most important to use wood wool that is both soft and fine with fibres that will break easily if the dog's legs become entangled in it. Wood shavings are also ideal, especially when used in quantities sufficient to allow the dog to make a hollow and still leave a 4–6in (10–15cm) depth to the floor. Shavings are excellent as long as there is no danger of entanglement and no dust, and are convenient as they come in compressed bale form. We have used shavings as summer bedding for quite some time and have found this choice to be free of most of the problems associated with other bedding. We sprinkle it with a mild, fragrant antiseptic before use to help keep the kennels and dogs smelling sweet.

Shredded paper is another excellent bedding material. It can also be purchased in a compressed bale, or you could buy a second-hand shredder quite cheaply to produce your own. Do not use colour magazine paper as some of the inks used for this purpose can be toxic. Also note that if your main source of paper is newspaper, then the newsprint may discolour the dog, especially if he is a lighter shade of fawn. Grooming or washing will, of course, soon remove this.

Sawdust is definitely not recommended for bedding. It gets into the dog's food, and into his eyes, ears, nose, and coats. We used to use sawdust many years ago until a speck of it got into the eye of one of our puppies. She subsequently had to undergo minor surgery to remove it as a new film had developed and trapped it on the lens overnight. Damp sawdust can also become compacted between the dog's footpads and toes, which if it was to go unnoticed would certainly cause future problems.

Ch. Amber Strike of Parabull (by Ch. Graecia Mercury, out of Helrouen Morgana Faye).

Cleaning

As most bedding materials are a haven for fleas and harmful bacteria, they should be replaced at least weekly. All dirty bedding materials can either be burned or disposed of quite easily. Beds should be removed and thoroughly cleaned, then washed with a correctly mixed solution of a good-quality proprietary disinfectant or bleach. The beds must then be rinsed in warm water and left to dry.

In general disinfectants are more effective when used at high temperatures, and even more so after organic matter has been removed and all surfaces cleaned thoroughly. Care should always be taken when handling or mixing disinfectants, and it is strongly recommended that you wear gloves, a mask, and eye protection at all times. Utensils used with such cleaners should be kept solely for this purpose.

The inside of the kennel should also be cleaned with disinfectant, although it is not advisable to wet it quite as thoroughly as the beds, especially if the kennel is of a wooden construction. Runs should be hosed and cleaned every day and thoroughly disinfected at least once a week. Feeding bowls should be disinfected with diluted Jeyes Fluid once a week, then rinsed thoroughly in warm water.

Finally, when there is a litter of puppies on your premises we strongly recommend that you provide a method for making sure that visitors do not bring in infection. The best way to do this is to provide a tray containing a mat or sponge soaked in disinfectant, onto which a visitor is asked to step before entering.

Exercise

Exercise is extremely important for all dogs whatever their age, both for their physical and mental well-being. The amount of exercise needed will vary from dog to dog. A fit, healthy dog in hard muscular condition should have no difficulty with reasonable amounts of exercise; on the contrary, he should look forward to it and enjoy it. It is quite easily within the capabilities of a fit Bullmastiff to manage 5–6 miles (8–10km) of vigorous exercise at any one time.

Exercise should be started slowly and increased gradually as the dog becomes fitter, stronger, and more able to cope. For the first week or two a steady walk on a lead of about 1½ miles (2.5km) twice a day should be sufficient. Over the next four to five weeks, providing the dog is showing no signs of distress, this can then gradually be increased to 2 miles (3km) twice a day, and at the same time the dog can be exercised for short distances over rough terrain. By the end of this time the dog should be fit enough to be allowed to run free, providing it is safe for him to do so.

There are many things that need to be taken into account before an exercise area can be considered safe. The first is that the area is securely fenced, as you don't want your dog escaping. When you take him out you must make yourself aware of the country code. The most important rule is that you must not allow your dog off the lead on farmland, especially in close proximity to livestock. A farmer is well within his rights to shoot a dog if he is worrying livestock. Another serious consideration is to make sure there has been no crop or weed spraying, as such chemicals can be fatal to dogs. Similarly, check that there are no poisonous plants or shrubs in the area. If the land you use for exercising your dog is not common land, always seek permission first, and avoid all children's play areas.

Do not be tempted to set the dog free right at the beginning of the exercise session, but walk him on a lead for a few minutes to allow his muscles to warm up first. This will reduce the risk of injury, and will stretch the muscles, ligaments, and tendons gently.

Remember that the Bullmastiff is a working dog and should therefore be quite capable of running, turning, twisting, and jumping without the risk of serious injury. This breed was developed for a specific purpose, and dogs were expected to work all night regardless of weather conditions, jumping gates, hedges, and walls to defend the gamekeeper against poachers and their dogs. You should not therefore wrap your dog in cotton wool with the sole intention of avoiding injuries just for the sake of the show ring. He deserves more from life than being treated as a precious statue.

A dog needs exercising over many surfaces and terrains to stay in tip-top condition. The effort needed to climb up hills will greatly improve the muscle development of the hindquarters, while the resistance used when going downhill enhances the muscle development of the forequarters. Hard, uneven surfaces tighten and improve the feet immensely. If you have more than one dog try to exercise them in pairs, as not only is this easier and more convenient but it has the added advantage that the dogs can run and play together. After the initial half-mile or so of walking on their leads, release the dogs and allow them the freedom to explore and to romp and play together while you take things more gently. In this way your dogs will end up covering at least two or three times the ground that you do.

6

Showing

Having come through the first few months unscathed, now is the time to put your plans of showing your dog to the test. In this chapter we give you a brief insight into the show scene. However, before we do so we would like to impress upon you the fact that you will lose more often than you win. If you are the type of person who cannot lose gracefully, then showing is not for you.

To ascertain whether you are likely to enjoy showing and to gauge whether you have the mental aptitude for it, attend several shows before you start showing yourself. At the same time you can compare mentally the attributes of your puppy to those present. Talk to as many of the exhibitors as possible, and take note of how the various handlers exhibit their dogs. You will no doubt hear criticisms of the dogs being shown and probably of the judge as well, but do not be unduly influenced by this. Remember that all written standards are open to individual interpretations. Providing the various observations of the particular dogs in question are based on a sound knowledge of the breed and are constructive, then they all have an acceptable place in the show scene.

Types of Show

There are many different classifications of shows throughout the UK, ranging from exemption shows and match meetings, through sanction, limited, and open shows to championship shows. Exemption shows are, as the name suggests, exempt from most of the regulations that apply to the other types of show. You do, however, require a Kennel Club licence to conduct such a show, and the show may include only a maximum of five pedigree classes. Match meetings are usually organized by general canine societies, most of which allow entries to be taken on the day. As the name implies, they often take the form of a knock-out competition. Individual clubs sometimes compete at match meetings, and they tend to have a very relaxed atmosphere.

Breed-only sanction shows usually schedule up to ten classes, the highest of which may be no higher than Post Graduate. Limited shows are strictly limited to members of the organizing club or society, and must include an Open class. Only dogs that have not yet gained an award counting towards the title of Champion (for example, Challenge Certificates or Green Stars) are eligible to enter a limited show. Open shows are open to any dog, regardless of his previous wins. Championship shows are much the same as the open shows, in as much as any dog can compete. The winning exhibit of each sex is awarded a Kennel Club Challenge Certificate. All shows except exemption shows are subject to Kennel Club rules and regulations, and organizers have to obtain a licence to conduct such a show from The Kennel Club.

Always start at the bottom with the small shows, then slowly, as you and your puppy become more confident, progress up the scale. It is a long, hard, and sometimes tedious journey to win at a championship show, but although many never reach this goal most people enjoy the time spent trying.

Show Classes

At the smaller shows there may only be four classes scheduled, such as Puppy dog or bitch, Junior dog or bitch, Post Graduate dog or bitch, and Open dog or bitch. Unfortunately, such a classification allows little scope for dogs that are too old to compete in Puppy or Junior classes but have yet to mature sufficiently to compete in the Open class. Bitches in particular seem to be at a disadvantage with this very restricted classification.

A slightly larger show may very well have a better classification, with Puppy dog, Puppy bitch, Junior dog, Junior bitch, Novice dog or bitch, Post Graduate dog or bitch, and Open dog and Open bitch. This classification is much better balanced and tends to give equal opportunities to both sexes. It also encourages those dogs that are over age for the younger classes yet not ready for the Open classes.

For your help and information, The Kennel Club definitions of the classes most often scheduled for the breed are given below. There are, of course, many other classifications, details of which will be supplied by The Kennel Club on request along with a copy of its show regulations. (Classes indicated with an asterisk are found only at open and championship shows.)

Minor Puppy For dogs of six and not exceeding nine calendar months of age on the first day of the show.

Puppy For dogs of six and not exceeding twelve calendar months of age on the first day of the show.

Junior For dogs of six and not exceeding eighteen calendar months of age on the first day of the show.

Special *Yearling* For dogs of six and not exceeding twenty-four calendar months of age on the first day of the show.

Maiden* For dogs that have not won a Challenge Certificate or a first prize at an open or championship show (Minor Puppy, Special Minor Puppy, Puppy, and Special Puppy classes excepted, whether restricted or not). Also for dogs that have not won a first prize at any show (Minor Puppy, Special Minor Puppy, Puppy, and Special Puppy classes excepted, whether restricted or not).

Novice* For dogs that have not won a Challenge Certificate or three or more first prizes at open and championship shows (Minor Puppy, Special Minor Puppy, Puppy, and Special Puppy classes excepted, whether restricted or not). Also for dogs that have not won three or more first prizes at any show (Minor Puppy, Special Minor Puppy, Puppy, and Special Puppy classes excepted, whether restricted or not).

Tyro* For dogs that have not won a Challenge Certificate or five or more first prizes at open and championship shows (Minor Puppy, Special Minor Puppy, Puppy, and Special Puppy classes excepted, whether restricted or not). Also for dogs that have not won five or more first prizes at any show (Minor Puppy, Special Minor Puppy, Puppy, and Special Puppy classes excepted, whether restricted or not).

Débutante* For dogs that have not won a Challenge Certificate or a first prize at a championship show (Minor Puppy, Special Minor Puppy, Puppy, and Special Puppy classes excepted, whether restricted or not). Also for dogs that have not won a first prize at an open or championship show (Minor Puppy, Special Minor Puppy, Puppy, and Special Puppy classes excepted, whether restricted or not).

Graduate* For dogs that have not won a Challenge Certificate or four or more first prizes at championship shows in Graduate, Post Graduate, Minor Limit, Mid Limit, Limit, and Open classes, whether restricted or not. Also for dogs that have not won four or more first prizes at open or championship shows in Graduate, Post Graduate, Minor Limit, Mid Limit, Limit, and Open classes, whether restricted or not.

Post Graduate* For dogs that have not won a Challenge Certificate or five or more first prizes at championship shows in Post Graduate, Minor Limit, Mid Limit, Limit, and Open classes, whether restricted or not. Also for dogs that have not won five or more first prizes at championship and open shows in Post Graduate, Minor Limit, Mid Limit, Limit, and Open classes, whether restricted or not.

Limit* For dogs that have not won three Challenge Certificates under three different judges or seven or more first prizes in all, at championship shows in Limit and Open classes, confined to the breed, whether restricted or not, at shows where Challenge Certificates were offered for the breed. Also for dogs that have not won seven or more first prizes in all at open and championship shows in Limit and Open classes, confined to the breed, whether restricted or not.

Ch. Bunsoro Proud Mary, (owner by Dr R. James) who won the bitch CC at Crufts 1981.

Open For all dogs of the breeds for which the class is provided and that are eligible for entry at the show. Wins at championship shows in breed classes where Challenge Certificates are not on offer shall be counted as wins at open shows.

While it is possible to enter at any show without gaining prior qualifications, to enter at Crufts, The Kennel Club's own championship show, various qualifications do need to be attained, usually in the year prior to the show. These requirements are continually reviewed by The Kennel Club in the interest of maintaining high standards. The exceptions are if the dog has won a Challenge Certificate or Reserve Challenge Certificate, or has gained entry into The Kennel Club Stud Book.

For a dog to be awarded the title of Champion, he must have been awarded three Challenge Certificates by three different judges, at least one of which must be awarded over the age of twelve months.

Preliminaries

Most shows are advertised in the dog press. To enter a show you must first obtain a schedule from the show secretary. The schedule provides all the relevant details and classifications for your breed plus an entry form. Send the completed entry form with a cheque or postal order to the secretary before the closing date. It is always good practice to include a stamped self-addressed envelope or postcard which the secretary can return to you as proof that your entry has been received.

Showing is restricted to dogs over six months of age that have been registered with The Kennel Club and transferred into your ownership. It is, however, possible to show before all the paperwork has been completed, provided that you add 'NAF' (name applied for) and/or 'TAF' (transfer applied for) after the dog's name on the entry form. To avoid these problems in the first place complete the section for transfer of ownership on the reverse side of the puppy's registration certificate as soon as you receive it from the breeder.

Show Training

Training for the show ring should start at a very early age, usually after all inoculations are completed. One of the first things that is necessary is to teach the puppy to stand still; this is quite easily achieved during the puppy's daily walk without him being aware that he is being trained. Periodically stop during the walk and at the same time give the command 'Stand'. Encourage the puppy to do so, and even if he manages to stand for only for a few seconds, praise and reward him, then continue on your walk. If you repeat this process two or three times during each walk and slowly increase the amount of time the puppy stands, then in a very short time he will stand still when commanded.

The next step is to teach him to stand in the desired stance. This can best be achieved by positioning one of the puppy's feet at a time whilst he is standing still. Gradually place all the feet in their correct positions so as to give the square appearance of the Bullmastiff. It is not usual at this stage to expect the puppy to stand perfectly square, and as long as he is quite happy for you to move and place his feet then it is no problem if he moves them a few seconds after you have done so. With repetition he will learn to resettle his balance and leave his feet where you place them, and soon after to stand naturally by himself in the correct position. It will, however, take time and patience on your part, but with plenty of verbal encouragement and the occasional reward you will soon have a puppy that is a pleasure to handle.

Once your puppy has mastered the art of standing correctly on command, he is ready to learn to allow people to run their hands over him, just as a judge would do. Start very gradually during play times by looking at his teeth, lifting his head, and running your hands over his body and legs. Next, set your puppy up in his show stance at every opportunity and ask family and friends to go over him, examining him as if they were judging him. To start with he will probably attempt to join in the fun, but if you are firm but kind with him he will soon accept it all quite happily.

It would be of great benefit at this stage to attend a ringcraft club; these are organized mainly by exhibitors for exhibitors. Here you will learn all the basic rudiments needed to train you and your puppy for the next big step in your show quest. Ringcraft clubs are advertised at veterinary surgeries, local libraries, and in some pet stores, or failing this a list of registered ringcraft clubs can be obtained from The Kennel Club. There are usually people at such classes who can offer help and advice on all aspects of showing. It is most important not only to attend these classes on a regular basis, but also to practise what you learn as often as possible at home.

Having familiarized your puppy with the routines of standing and allowing people to go over him, the next serious lesson is to teach him to move on a loose lead and at the correct speed. Your puppy must learn to move at a collected trot, as at this speed the judge will

Ch. Zeela of Oldwell.

be able to assess good or bad movement and thereby confirm in general the dog's construction. At most shows you will be requested to move your dog in a triangle. When you do so remember that you must always have your puppy on your left side, and must never block the judge's view of your dog either when standing or on the move. The first leg of the triangle sees the puppy moving away from the judge, thus allowing him or her to evaluate the rear movement. The second part of the triangle presents the side view of the dog, allowing the judge to assess the reach and flexing of both front and rear quarters. The third stage of the triangle demonstrates the front movement head on.

Practice of these skills comes easily to a puppy who loves to walk with you. To deter him from moving too fast or jumping during the collected trot, pull back gently on the lead, and again be firm and kind. Talk him through the lessons and encourage him to enjoy them, all the while treating him, praising him, and encouraging him to be happy so that you form a natural bond. He should enjoy the show so that he steps out proudly, eyes sparkling, tail wagging, and with a movement that is just so.

Presentation

A dog that is well turned out will always catch the eye of any judge, so it is essential to pay particular attention to grooming beforehand. Brush your dog thoroughly, then just before you enter the ring wipe his coat over with either a chamois leather or a piece of silk to give it that extra sheen.

While they are out exercising Bullmastiffs appear to go out of their way to find mud and dirty puddles to roll in. If this happens just before a show the only solution is to bath him. There are numerous shampoos and conditioners available, but don't go to any great expense as Bullmastiffs have a short, hard, weatherproof coat that requires very little in the way of bathing. Be sure to rinse thoroughly to remove all traces of shampoo, then allow him to shake himself, making sure you stand well clear. Using rough towels, give him a good rub-down to ensure he is completely dry. If for any reason you need to wash him prior to a show, try to do so at least three days in advance so that all loose hairs can be brushed out and some of the natural oils of the coat can have time to return.

Austral. Ch. Nightkeeper Arni.

Dress for the show ring to complement your dog. Gentlemen should wear neat trousers, with a shirt or sweater and comfortable shoes. Ladies should choose a smart dress, or a skirt or trousers, with a blouse or sweater, again with comfortable, flat-heeled shoes. Ensure your shoes afford good grip so that you are less likely to slip on a polished floor, wet grass, or mud. Try to dress in contrasting colours to your dog; it is difficult for a judge to assess the outline of a fawn dog against a background of beige clothes, and even more difficult to assess a brindle dog against black ones. Never wear clothes that are so loose that they flap about and distract the dogs.

At the Show

You should always arrive at the show with plenty of time to spare before judging starts. Give yourself time to park the car, and to find your way with your bags and dogs from the car-park to the benches.

Make it a policy to be at the show and settled down with your dog at least half a hour before judging is due to commence. Be extra vigilant at the entrance to the venue, for it is here, where there are large numbers of dogs confined in a small area, that the occasional squabble between dogs may occur.

After you have found your dog's bench and settled him on it, leave a reliable person in charge so that you can go and collect your catalogue and locate the ring in which your breed is to show. The best thing you can do now, after all the hustle and bustle of getting there, is to sit down and relax for a few minutes with a cup of tea. Take your dog to the exercise area provided before he is due in the ring to allow him time to relieve himself.

It is not advisable to feed your dog just prior to leaving for a show. If he is not used to travelling long distances then doing so with a

Int. Ch. Graecia Rhapsody.

heavy meal in his stomach could cause him to vomit, and the poor dog would feel out of sorts and lack his usual self-confidence. A second reason for not feeding beforehand is that some dogs tend to lose their natural sparkle after a feed. If you need to attract your dog with a titbit whilst showing then it stands to reason that he will be more attentive if he is slightly hungry.

When you start showing even match meetings appear daunting, so relax and try to treat them as a further training session. Don't be embarrassed about making mistakes as the majority of exhibits at these meetings tend to be puppies and young stock, all equally new to the game; in any case, even the most experienced of handlers make mistakes with youngsters.

Most of the smaller shows follow a very similar pattern to the procedure used at ringcraft classes. At the show each exhibit will be allocated a number, which will be the number of your dog as printed in the catalogue. More often than not the ring steward will hand this number to you as you enter the ring, although you may be expected to collect it from the secretary before judging commences. The number must be displayed on your person whilst you are in the ring with your dog. The most usual method for this is to attach it with a pin or

Ch. Bournvalley Misty of Meitza.

a ring clip specially made for the purpose, although it is becoming more common to fix the number to your sleeve with tapes or an elastic band.

Once you are in the ring position yourself and your dog in the line of exhibits, taking care that you do not in any way obstruct the exhibits on either side of you and that they in turn do not obstruct you, and keeping a reasonable space between yourself and the nearest exhibitor. The normal procedure is for the judge to ask each exhibitor to stand his dog separate from the rest. The judge will then examine and assess the dog, and ask the handler to move him so that he may evaluate the movement of the dog.

After all the dogs in the class have been assessed in this way the judge will place them in order of merit. Usually at an open show the places are first, second, third, and reserve, while at a championship show it is normal for the first five or six dogs to be placed in order of merit. This procedure is carried out for each class scheduled. If the scheduled classes are of mixed sexes then all the unbeaten exhibits will be brought back into the ring at the end, and from these the judge will select a Best in Breed. For Reserve Best in Breed the judge may ask for any dog that has only been beaten by the Best in Breed to be brought back into the ring together with the other unbeaten dogs, and he will then select his winner from these. Best Puppy is selected from all puppies that have not been previously beaten by another puppy.

At championship shows the classes are scheduled for each sex, and the general procedure for each class is the same as for open shows. After all the dog classes have been judged the unbeaten dogs are brought into the ring, and from these the judge will select his Best Dog. If the judge considers that this dog is worthy of the award then he or she will present him with the Challenge Certificate. The Reserve Best Dog will be selected from the remaining unbeaten dogs along with any dog that has only been beaten by the Best Dog. Exactly the same procedure is followed for the bitches. Having selected the Best Dog and Best Bitch, the judge will choose the Best in Breed from these. The Reserve Best in Breed will then be selected from the Best Opposite Sex and the Reserve of the same sex as the Best in Breed. After this has been completed the judge will select the Best Puppy from the winners of all the puppy classes along with any puppy that has not been beaten by another puppy. If a puppy should win Best in Breed or Reserve Best in Breed then obviously he would automatically be Best Puppy.

*Austral. & Mal. Ch.
Lilacglen the Legend.*

All of the Best in Breed winners from each breed go forward to the group judging, where the judge will select four exhibits in order of merit. This is repeated for each group, and from these winners the Best in Show and Reserve Best in Show are selected. The same procedures are conducted to select the Best Puppy in Show and the Reserve Best Puppy in Show.

All the time you are in the ring put into practice the skills you have learned at the ringcraft training classes. Show your dog to his best possible advantage – if this means showing him in profile, then do so, or if his best feature is his front then show him front on to the judge. That said, you must be prepared to exhibit the dog in whichever position the judge requests, as he or she naturally has the final word.

118

Never stop showing until the judge has made his final decision – there are many instances of a judge reversing his decision after a final look down the line. Finally, always feel confident and at ease in the ring as this will boost your puppy's confidence.

Showing Around the World

Australia

Although some of the classes at shows in Australia differ from those in the UK, each individual class is judged in a very similar manner. All dog classes are judged first, then the winners of each class (with the exception of the Baby Puppy class) are brought into the ring where the judge selects the Challenge Winner. The Reserve Challenge Winner is then selected from the balance of class-winning exhibits and the second-place winner from the class in which the Challenge Winner was entered. The same procedures are repeated to arrive at the bitch Challenge Winner and Reserve Challenge Winner. The Best in Breed is decided between the Challenge Winner dog and Challenge Winner bitch. The Runner-Up Best in Breed is then selected from the unsuccessful Challenge Winner in the Best in Breed competition and Reserve Challenge Winner.

Austral. Ch. Treebrook Silver Wattle.

119

Mr Keith Warren with NZ Ch. Oakcroft First Edition, NZ Ch. Silver Lisa of Mors, and Graecia Thunder 'n' Lightning.

The Australian system varies from the UK system mainly in that each class is awarded a winner. This is arrived at by selecting a winner from the class winners of each sex. For example, the dog and bitch winners of the Open class will be brought together for the judge to decide the better of the two, which will then be declared the Best in Breed of Class. This same procedure is followed for all classes except those from which the Best in Breed and Runner-Up Best in Breed came, provided the Best in Breed winner was not entered in the same class.

For a dog to be awarded the title of Champion, he must have been awarded a total of 100 challenge points gained at no fewer than four championship shows, and under no fewer than four different judges at different shows. Challenge points are only awarded to exhibits aged over six months. A dog Challenge Certificate winner is awarded five points, while one point is allocated to each dog of the same breed exhibited that is over six months of age. The same scale applies for the bitches. The winner in each of the six groups is awarded five points, while one point goes to each dog and bitch exhibited in the group. A dog that wins Best in Show at an all-breeds show is awarded twenty-five points. A dog that wins Best in Show at a specialist show is awarded five points, while one point is allocated to each dog and bitch exhibited. Other than Best in Show at an all-breeds show, wins cannot accumulate and the number of points cannot exceed twenty-five in any one show.

New Zealand

Ribbon parades are informal shows open to all pedigree dogs, very similar to our match meetings, and as such can be good practice for both handlers and dogs. It is possible to enter on the day, and owners are not required to be members of The New Zealand Kennel Club (NZKC). Champion dogs may only compete in Stakes classes.

SA Ch. Kim Ken Shea of Starvalley, Bullmastiff of the Year (SA) from 1989 to 1994, and winner of ninety-nine Best of Breed and five Best of Show titles.

At open shows owners must be members of the NZKC and all dogs must be registered with the organization. Dogs must be entered prior to the show, and no Challenge Certificates are awarded. At championship shows dogs must also be entered in advance and all owners must be members of the NZKC. Obviously, Challenge Certificates are awarded at these shows.

Each dog class is judged and the dogs are placed first, second, third, and reserve in order of merit. The winners of each of these classes are then brought back into the ring to compete for Best Dog, after which the dog placed in his class second to the Best Dog is again brought back into the ring to compete with the remaining class winners for Reserve Best Dog. At a championship show these dogs would normally be the Dog Challenge Certificate winner and the Reserve Dog Challenge Certificate winner. The same procedure is carried out to arrive at the Best Bitch and the Reserve Best Bitch, or in the case of a championship show, the Bitch Challenge Certificate winner and Reserve Bitch Challenge Certificate winner.

The Best Dog and Best Bitch are judged to decide the Best in Breed. The Reserve of Sex of the Best in Breed can then compete with the Best of Opposite Sex for Reserve Best in Breed. The winners of the Baby Puppy classes in each sex are then judged to decide the Best Baby Puppy. This procedure is applied through all the classes scheduled.

All Best in Breed winners from a particular group are then judged to decide Best in Group. The Reserve Best in Breed winner to the Best in Group winner is then allowed to compete along with all other Best in Breed winners for Reserve Best in Group. All Best in Group winners compete for Best in Show. The Reserve from the winner's group can compete with other group winners for Reserve Best in Show.

The Best in Class winners are judged in a similar way to decide Best Baby Puppy in Group, and so on through all the classes. In these groups there are no Reserves in Groups. The group winners for these particular classes are then judged to decide the Best in Class for each class in the show; again, there are no Reserves.

To qualify for the title of New Zealand Champion a dog has to be awarded eight Challenge Certificates by at least five different judges. Puppies (aged six to twelve months) can be awarded Challenge Certificates but at least one of the eight must have been awarded when the dog was over the age of twelve months if he is to qualify as a champion. Baby Puppies are not eligible to compete for Challenge Certificates.

Southern Africa

Only Bullmastiffs registered with The Kennel Union of Southern Africa (KUSA) may be shown at KUSA shows. There are two types of show: non-championship, or open, shows and championship shows. At non-championship shows puppies from the age of four months may be shown, while at championship shows dogs must be over six months old and all entries have to be submitted in advance of the show date.

Any dog that wins a class goes forward with the winners of the other classes for that sex to compete for the Challenge Certificate. The two Challenge Certificate winners, together with the unbeaten prize winners of any restricted class (for example, Champions), go forward to be judged Best in Breed. The Best in Breeds from each group advance to the group judging, and the Best in Group then advance to the judging of Best in Show. A similar advancement is made for Best Puppy in Show. Reserve awards are only made at Challenge Certificate and Best in Breed levels. Although it is not required by KUSA regulations, a number of clubs give awards for Best Opposite Sex.

In order to be granted championship status a dog must have achieved a minimum of five points in any combination of one- and two-point Challenge Certificates. (Two-point CCs are only available when ten or more dogs of a breed/sex are exhibited at a show.) For the purposes of awarding Challenge Certificates the region is divided into eleven centres, and of the minimum five points not more than four of these can have been awarded in any one centre. Where the points are won has nothing to do with the residence of the owner, exhibitor, or dog, but rests purely on the location of the centre where the show is held. CCs awarded before a dog is nine months old do not count towards Champion status. At least one CC must have been awarded after a dog is eighteen months old, and all the CCs submitted as evidence of qualifying for championship status must have been awarded by different judges.

Canada

The judge begins each show with the Junior Puppy Male class, evaluates each dog, and awards first, second, third, and fourth placings. Judging proceeds through Senior Male Puppy class, the Twelve to Eighteen Months class, the Canadian-Bred class, the Bred-by-

Fin. Ch. Dogmatic Axl W. Rose, Bullmastiff of the Year (Finland) 1996.

Exhibitor class, and the Open class. After all the male classes have been judged the winners of each class are brought back into the ring to compete for the Winners Male award. The dog placed second in the class from which the Winners Male is chosen is then brought back into the ring to compete against the other class winners for Reserve Winners Male. The Veteran class is then judged, and the whole process repeated for bitches.

Specials Only are champions of record. All dogs entered in Specials Only are brought into the ring with the Veteran Male class winner, the Veteran Female class winner, the Winners Male, and the Winners Female for the selection of Best in Breed and Best of Opposite Sex to Best in Breed. The Best of Winners is selected between the Winners Male and the Winners Female. If the Winners Male or Winners Female is awarded Best in Breed, that dog is automatically Best of Winners. After the Best of Winners award, the judge selects the Best Puppy in Breed from the undefeated puppies in the competition.

On the completion of all Best in Breed judging, the Best in Breed dogs are brought into the ring and the judge awards first, second, third, and fourth in group. Following this, Best Puppy in Breed winners are judged for Best Puppy in Group. From the winners of each group the judge selects Best in Show. The same procedure is followed for Best Puppy in Show.

To qualify for the title of Champion a dog has to earn at least ten championship points under at least three different judges, and must be individually registered in the records of The Canadian Kennel Club (CKC) or have an event registration number. The number of points that a dog is able to win is determined by the number of dogs competing for those points.

If a dog awarded Winners is also awarded Best in Breed, then all dogs competing in the breed shall be included in the total. If a dog awarded Winners is also awarded Best Opposite Sex, then all dogs of the same sex shall be included in the total. If a dog awarded Winners is also awarded Best of Winners then all dogs defeated directly or indirectly in the breed shall be included in the total. If a dog is awarded Winners only, then all the dogs of the same sex in the class competition shall be included in the total.

In addition to points allocated at breed level, a dog awarded Winners that is also placed in the regular group competition shall be credited with further points (to a maximum of five), once again according to the number of dogs competing at group level.

United States

There are six different regular classes, offered for male and female dogs separately in each breed entered at a show. The winners of each male class compete for the best of the winning dogs, and the process is repeated for female classes. Only the best male (Winners Dog) and the best female (Winners Bitch) receive championship points. A Reserve Winner award is given in each sex to the runner-up.

The Winners Dog and the Winners Bitch then compete with the champions for Best in Breed. At the end of the Best in Breed competition three awards are usually given: Best in Breed (the dog judged as the best in its breed category); Best of Winners (the dog judged as best between the Winners Dog and Winners Bitch); and Best of Opposite Sex (the best dog of the opposite sex to the Best in Breed winner). The Best in Breed winners then advance to compete in the group, where four places are awarded. The winners of each group compete for Best in Show.

To qualify for the title of American Kennel Club (AKC) Champion a dog must be awarded fifteen points, including two majors (wins of three, four, or five points) under at least three different judges. A dog can earn up to five points towards the Champion title at any one show.

The Netherlands

To qualify for the title of Dutch Champion the dog has to obtain four points in total. This can be reached with single points and double points. Single points are allocated with the following: a Championship Award (CAC) at a championship show; a Reserve Championship Award at a championship club match; or four or more Reserve Championship Awards at shows. Double points are given for a Championship Award at the Winner in Amsterdam and a Championship Award at a championship club match. Note that a Championship Award can only count double once!

On the day he gains his last (Reserve) Championship Award, the dog should be at least twenty-seven months old. If the dog has obtained enough points before the age of twenty-seven months then he needs only to obtain a Reserve Championship Award after this age to qualify for Champion status. The (Reserve) Championship Awards must be judged by at least two different judges. Finally, in order to qualify the dog has to be registered in a stud book recognized by the Fédération Cynologique Internationale (FCI) for at least one generation.

7

Judging and Stewarding

It is an honour and privilege to be invited to judge at any level, and should be accepted as such. For the majority of judges such an opportunity comes only after many years of active involvement with the breed. When you are invited to judge, you should do so with honesty and integrity, and carry out your job in a professional manner. This may sound simple and straightforward, but it is amazing how many judges conduct themselves in a completely unprofessional manner, making the most elementary mistakes in ring procedure and appearing not to follow a set method of examining and assessing the exhibits. As a judge it is your responsibility to be completely impartial and unbiased at all times. First and foremost you are there to judge the dogs.

It is extremely important when judging that you pay attention to what you wear. Clothing should be comfortable and smart, but not overdone. It is only common sense that your apparel should not be loose and flap about to the extent that it frightens younger exhibits, but nor should it be so tight as to restrict your movements. Shoes should be smart and comfortable, and should also be suited to inclement weather conditions if you are working outdoors.

Judging Procedure

It is usual to introduce yourself to the stewards as soon as possible, and to discuss with them the manner in which you would like them to organize the exhibits and the ring. Make sure they know your requirements before judging commences.

After the steward has informed you that all the exhibits for a particular class are in the ring and are ready, commence by having a general look at the exhibits as they stand in line. Ask each of the exhibitors to stand their dog in the designated place within the ring, allowing them sufficient time in which to set up their dog. Never be

Ch. Naukeen Lorraine (right), and Ch. Pekintown Abece.

in so much of a hurry that you begin to encroach on the handler. Be courteous to all exhibitors at all times, and when giving them instructions be precise.

Have a set routine for examining each exhibit and stick to it; if you are haphazard in your approach you may forget to assess a particular feature. When handling puppies be gentle yet firm, as rough handling at such an early age by a judge can spoil a young puppy's future show career.

Normally a detailed assessment of the dog starts by gaining his attention, and whilst he is alert assessing the ears for colour, size, and carriage. Lift the head and examine the eyes for colour, shape, size, and placement, and follow this by checking the stop. Proceed from there to the muzzle, paying particular attention to the bone structure (it is quite common for some dogs, especially those with a shorter muzzle, to have an abundance of flesh over the muzzle but very little bone under this). From here check the dentition. Before leaving the head evaluate the balance of the skull to foreface and muzzle, and lastly check the pigmentation.

Assess the neck, and from there check the placement of the shoulders and length of the humerus. Check the front: are the legs straight and the pasterns firm? At the same time assess the depth and width of the chest. Moving back, check the spring and length of the ribcage, the width of the loin, and the depth of the flank. At the hindquarters check angulation, firmness, and muscle tone, and last but not least examine the tail.

Having finished the hands-on assessment, stand back, take a final look at the overall appearance of the dog, and then request the handler to move the exhibit to your requirements. Movement in a triangle will enable you to assess the dog's rear movement, then when he is in profile to assess front and rear extension, head and neck carriage, and whether or not the dog maintains his topline, and finally his front movement as he comes back towards you. You may also instruct an exhibitor to move in a circle or in a straight line away from you and back again.

After you have assessed each exhibit place them in order of merit. Don't dither over this, but be definite in your decisions. The steward will usually hand you your judge's book so that you can record your placings and, if required, take notes for your critique. As a judge remember that you must always assess each exhibit in relation to the Standard and not to personal preferences.

The Judge's Critique

After each show in the UK, whatever its size, judges are requested to write a critique for the winning exhibits. At an open show a judge must write a critique for the first place only and simply name the second and third places, while at a championship show and breed club open show he or she is expected to write a critique for the first- and second-placed exhibits and to name the third. At Crufts judges are expected to write a critique for the first three places in every class. Although it is not compulsory for a judge to undertake to write a critique, it is fast becoming a stipulation of many societies that on acceptance of an appointment a judge agrees to this request.

When writing a critique you must be relatively brief yet also descriptive. Remember that it not only gives your opinion of the dog, but must also provide a description of the dog for those who have not seen him at first hand. If, in your opinion, a particular dog has a superb head or an excellent front, or if any other part of the animal deserves praise, then you should say so. By the same rule, if you consider a dog weak in a particular department then you must also comment on this.

Qualifications for Judging

Different countries require different qualifications for championship-level judges.

United Kingdom

At this moment The Kennel Club has no strict written criteria for assessing judges, but considers each applicant individually, taking into account all previous experience and in particular judging experience relating to the breed in question. Also considered is the applicant's total experience associated with dogs in general and in particular with the breed for which the application to award Challenge Certificates is relevant.

The Kennel Club does, however, insist that all those invited to judge should complete a questionnaire, which requests details of the applicant's judging experience – in other words, types of show judged, the number of classes, and the number of dogs. The questionnaire further requests information on the number of dogs of the relevant breed the applicant has bred or owned which have qualified for entry into The Kennel Club Stud Book, the number of champions or Challenge Certificate winners in the relevant breed either bred or owned by the applicant, stewarding experience, interest in breed clubs and any positions held in such clubs, attendance at seminars on the breed, and any other relevant experience.

On receiving such an application for a nominee The Kennel Club will invariably consult the relevant breed council to confirm that the applicant's name appears on the breed council's approved judging list. To qualify for inclusion on the Bullmastiff Breed Council's judging list of persons considered capable of awarding Challenge Certificates, a breed specialist must have owned a Bullmastiff and been active in the breed for a minimum period of five years. Following this he or she must have judged a minimum of 150 dogs over at least a five-year period and including at least one club show during that time (dogs entered yet not present do not count).

In the case of multi-breed judges (all-rounders) such criteria are not practical, and in these situations the Breed Council will consider the applicant's total experience in judging Bullmastiffs and details of breed seminars attended. The judging experience must include a club show and the nominee must be supported by that club.

Australia

Candidates are required to educate themselves to examination level by studying the Breed Standard, glossary of terms, and any other appropriate material. They should also research breeds and present

Miss Lilly Turner judging Ch. Doomwatch Gypsy of Oldwell (with Bronwyn Lucas) and Ch. Nicholas of Oldwell (with Harry Colliass).

131

their findings, attend appropriate lectures, seminars, and/or field days as arranged by the training committee, and acquire as wide a knowledge as possible by attending shows and obtaining breeders' opinions.

Judge's Training Programme   Applicants must have been a member of the Australian National Kennel Council (ANKC) for a minimum of eight years during the ten years immediately prior to the date of application. They must also have bred at least three litters under their own prefix, have made up and/or bred a minimum of two champions under their own prefix, and must have gained experience as a steward.

During the programme trainees are required to pass a written examination covering show rules and regulations and anatomy. In order to progress to championship level they must then judge a minimum of four groups or equivalent appointments (which should include a minimum of 100 exhibits), and must also attend at least one lecture on each breed in the group in the two-year period prior to the application, attend and pass the anatomy lecture, and pass both theoretical and practical examinations on the relevant breed.

New Zealand

To become a judge under New Zealand Kennel Club Judges' Regulations the applicant must have bred dogs for a minimum of three years and exhibited dogs for a minimum of six years, have been involved in club activities, performed minimum stewarding requirements, and have been approved by the Executive Council. Judges are then placed on a probationary list and, after sitting an examination, are permitted to join the Ribbon Parade Panel.

The New Zealand Kennel Club has a published panel, whose judges are only permitted to judge the breeds, groups, or Best in Shows for which they have qualifications. Judges can qualify for ribbon parades and open shows before they progress to the group panels. Both theoretical and practical examinations must be passed before judges are placed on the Championship Panel.

Southern Africa

Before a judge is allowed to set foot in a ring he must have been actively involved with dogs for a minimum of ten years, and must pass an examination on the rules and regulations appertaining to showing, canine conformation and movement, judging etiquette, and the Breed Standards of the breeds he wishes to judge. He is then allowed to judge at non-championship shows, at which he must submit written reports on the dogs he has judged. All identifying marks are then removed from the reports and they are sent to a panel of scrutineers who (with the possible exception of one) do not come from the area in which the judge resides.

Once a judge has examined sufficient specimens of a breed or breeds (where he is judging a number of breeds in a group, he must have judged those which are prevalent in the show ring), he then sits a more detailed examination on the breed or breeds he wishes to judge. When this has been passed he must judge sufficient exhibits at least twice at championship shows before he is placed on the panel for that breed or group. Once on the panel a judge is not required to sit further examinations. Finally, in order to judge at any event licensed by The Kennel Union of Southern Africa (KUSA), regardless of the discipline, a judge must be a current member of the Union.

Canada

Applicants to judge must have been a member of The Canadian Kennel Club (CKC) for five consecutive years immediately prior to

Ch. Dreadnot Melody Maker.

133

the application, and must also have been a resident of Canada during this period. They must have a minimum of ten years' breeding experience, during which time they must have bred a minimum of four Canadian-bred and CKC-registered litters, and must have bred and made up six CKC conformation champions. A CKC judge who is licensed for all breeds and who has a sound background in the breed for which the applicant is trying must act as a sponsor. The applicant must have judged a minimum of 150 dogs in, for example, sanction matches beforehand, and must have spent a minimum of sixty hours stewarding, attended seminars, workshops, and breed study groups, completed formal study courses, watched breed videos, visited prominent kennels, spent time with a mentor, and passed a written examination.

United States

The minimum requirements for an application to judge are ten years of documented experience, plus the ownership or exhibition of several dogs, the breeding of at least four litters, and the production of at least two champions. The applicant must also have stewarded at least five times, judged at least six times at matches sanctioned by The

Mrs Ruth Short of Bulstaff fame judging. Also in the picture are Bill Leedham (left) with Ch. Rommel of Ivywill, Jim Price (right, kneeling) of Lombardy Kennels, and Gerald Warren (background left) of Copperfield Kennels.

American Kennel Club (AKC), and have viewed the appropriate breed videos, and he or she must meet occupational eligibility requirements.

Although each of the systems for choosing judges in the countries discussed fulfils its purpose, it would appear to us that advantages from each could be combined to develop one that is superior to all of them. In our opinion the following criteria should apply. First, potential judges should have been involved in the dog scene for at least ten years. They should attend lectures and seminars, should read and understand the Breed Standard for the breed or breeds they hope to judge, and should have a knowledge of the anatomy of dogs in general. They should then be required to sit a written examination covering all these aspects.

This should then be followed by time spent judging at small shows or even assessing groups of dogs brought together for this purpose. At these events a total of at least 200 dogs of the breed should be assessed. After each event the prospective judges should give a written report detailing their decisions and the reasons for them. This would then be scrutinized by a selected panel of breed experts, all of whom should have many years' experience with the breed and have been approved to judge at championship level.

We do not believe that it is necessary for prospective judges to have bred a certain number of litters of the breed in question or have bred champions in this breed. There are excellent judges who have never owned a champion let alone bred one, and at the end of the day the most important experience for judging is gained through handling dogs and spending time assessing their varying virtues. This cannot be rushed, but is a long, gradual process of accumulating knowledge.

Stewarding

Although the judge is in sole control and ultimately responsible for the ring at all times, the stewards are there to help organize the ring for the judge. The stewards must be on hand at all times to assist both the judge and the exhibitors. In spite of all this, a good steward should remain as unobtrusive as possible during judging.

First the stewards must make sure that the ring is clean and clear of any objects that shouldn't be there. At least one of the stewards should go to the benching area to inform exhibitors when judging is about to commence. The steward within the ring must clearly announce the class to be judged by both name and number, and at the same time call for by number all the exhibits entered in that class. The steward must make sure the exhibitor clearly displays the dog's ring number at all times when in the ring, and furthermore must make note of any absentees from the class.

After first discussing with the judge procedures and where in the ring he or she would like the exhibits to be assembled, it is then the steward's responsibility to ask the exhibitors to form a line as directed, usually starting from the left-hand side of the judge's table. During judging the stewards must pay attention to the exhibitors, making sure that the next one is ready for the judge, and most importantly being on hand to deal with any problems that may arise. Stewards outside the ring are instructed to inform the judge if they witness anyone attracting the exhibits within the ring from the outside, and if so requested should then take steps to make sure that this behaviour ceases immediately.

At the end of each class the stewards must line up the class winners, starting with the first-place winner on the left to the last award on the right. They should then present each exhibitor with the relevant prize cards and rosettes. For all subsequent classes it is usually the accepted practice that the steward will assemble the exhibits entered in this class from an earlier class in the order in which the judge has previously placed them. After all classes for each sex have been judged the steward will call for unbeaten exhibits of that sex and place them in the ring in class-number order ready for the judge to award Best and Reserve of each sex. After Best in Breed has been decided it is the steward's responsibility to assemble all unbeaten puppies in the ring for the judge to select the Best Puppy.

8

Breeding

The prime reason why most people who are seriously involved with Bullmastiffs contemplate breeding is to try to produce a dog closer to their interpretation of the Standard. You should only breed to try to improve the quality of your stock; if you cannot improve, then don't breed. In our opinion anyone who breeds purely for financial gain will, in the long run, only cause damage to the breed.

Basic Genetics

While it is, of course, possible to breed good dogs that look the part and consequently achieve high honours in the show ring without a knowledge of genetics, such success is dependent on the many years' experience gained by the breeder. With a basic knowledge of genetics, however, this success can be achieved much sooner. As we are unqualified to give a detailed account of the workings of genetics, we recommend that anyone who is seriously interested in breeding dogs of a sound genetic make-up should read Malcolm B. Willis's book *Practical Genetics for Dog Breeders* (*see* Bibliography). We will nevertheless attempt to give a brief introduction to the very basic principles.

A dog's physical characteristics are governed by genes, which are inherited from his parents. Genes are either recessive or dominant, and are inherited in pairs, one coming from the dam and the other from the sire. The dominant gene of the pair will override the recessive gene, thereby making itself apparent in the offspring. Unfortunately, very few desirable characteristics are associated with a single gene; more often than not a specific group of genes will be responsible for them. Attempting to change one characteristic at the expense of another is not sound common sense, unless the other is of little importance.

From this simple explanation of the workings of heredity it will be observed that it is not the qualities displayed by the parents that are

137

Ch. Norwegian Wood of Rodekes.

passed on to the offspring as such, but the relationship of the genes that determines these qualities. The reason that a dog is similar to his ancestors is not that he is a part of the ancestors but that he shares with them a common gene pool, as will be any descendants. Following on from this, it will be clear that although the parents might appear outwardly normal, they might still 'carry' hidden a recessive gene for a deformity or mismark. The combination of such recessive genes will subsequently result in offspring that display these unwanted characteristics. Therefore, although you will have studied the stud-dog and brood-bitch along with their pedigrees, there is always the possibility that a small proportion of all litters will contain puppies with undesirable characteristics. In Bullmastiffs, these are most likely to be such conditions as light eyes, hare-lips, cleft palates, crank tails, umbilical hernias, timidity, aggression, entropion, ectropion, or white markings. It is only by careful mating and by keeping complete records of such matings, together with the records of all offspring produced and the use of deliberate test matings, that one is able to eradicate these problems.

An example of the rules of heredity at work can be seen in the colour of coats. It is generally accepted that the colour brindle is dominant to red or fawn, but not completely so. Breeders have stated in the past that if a brindle mated to either a red or fawn produces only brindles in the litter, then the brindle parent is completely dominant for the brindle colour. However, we do not believe that this holds true in all cases.

To substantiate our statement, we refer to an occasion when we mated a brindle to a fawn and all the resultant puppies were brindle. When the same mating was repeated at a later date half the puppies were brindle and half fawn. As brindle is dominant to fawn, this appears to indicate that the brindle parent must have been carrying a recessive gene for the colour fawn. Therefore, to be able to state with any confidence that a brindle is completely dominant for the colour brindle, this dog must only produce brindle puppies in *every* litter, whatever the colour of the partner. In fact, as there is a long-established custom of mating brindles to reds, or to fawns if no suitable red is available (many people fear that crossing two brindles will produce black puppies), we doubt very much that there are any brindles in the UK that are dominant in this colour.

In our early endeavours to breed Bullmastiffs we probably experienced nearly everything that could go wrong with the breed. Be that as it may, the better puppies we produced were of an excellent quality without the associated problems of the breed. With careful matings and selection we finally managed to achieve sound foundation stock. Although we learned a great deal from these experiences, we believe that had some of the earlier breeders been more open with their knowledge then perhaps most of the common deformities associated with Bullmastiffs could have been either eradicated or kept under control within fine limits many years ago. The betterment of any breed is based on openness and free discussion. Without such openness and honesty a breed may suffer for many more years than is necessary. If an exceptional dog or bitch should produce a puppy or puppies with a deformity then the pair should not automatically be discarded. Investigation may reveal how such a condition arose, and you can then take steps to breed litters that retain the excellence of the parents without the undesirable condition.

The art of breeding is to accept what you have, including all undesirable genes, then to try to improve for future generations. We were advised many years ago by a long-established breeder to learn from our mistakes as they are part of the price we pay for knowledge. And this advice still holds true today.

Breeding Systems

The various methods of breeding commonly used are inbreeding, line-breeding, outcrossing, and random breeding.

Inbreeding

This is mating together closely related animals, such as father to daughter, mother to son, brother to sister, and occasionally half-brother to half-sister. By its very nature inbreeding cannot bring fresh genes into the pool. However, it will in a very short time reveal not only the highly desirable genes carried by your stock, but also all the hidden horrors. It is the quickest and most direct method by which to fix characteristics in your stock. If you intend to inbreed you should be fully aware of the possible problems before you begin, and be prepared not only to accept these but also to deal with them as they occur.

There is a disdain for inbreeding amongst many breeders, who believe that it is not natural and therefore should not be practised. However, inbreeding is not only common but often the norm amongst herds or packs of wild animals. In such a situation the dominant male mates all the females, which will include his sisters and daughters. Eventually a younger male – perhaps his son – will assume the role of dominant sire and continue to mate the females, all of which he is closely related to as most of them will have been sired by his father. Thus the next generation will be even more closely inbred, and so it progresses through the generations, with only the dominant males having the opportunity to sire.

Contrary to popular belief such herds do not die out but are in fact vigorous as the weaker animals will already have been weeded out by Nature's rule of the survival of the fittest. The breeder should in

*Ch. Yorkist Magician of
Oldwell with Harry Colliass.*

effect take on the role of Mother Nature with regards to selection, to the extent that as in nature genetically unsound animals are not given the opportunity to breed.

The offspring resulting from inbreeding are more likely to be similar to their parents, in appearance and genetic make-up, in terms of both dominant and recessive characteristics. If inbreeding is carried on over the generations then the offspring will gradually become not only similar in appearance, but their genetic make-up will also become more similar; the longer it is continued the more will certain points – both good and bad – be fixed.

It is only by severe selection in each breeding generation that you will be able to reduce the unwanted combinations of genes. By so doing the stock produced will eventually be pure dominant or pure recessive for almost all of the characteristics, good or bad. Unwanted traits must be weeded out vigorously at every stage to enable the breeder to finish with genetically sound stock. In the beginning, the rejection figure may be as high as 90 per cent of all stock produced, although this number will reduce rapidly as you progress.

At the start of such a breeding programme the initial results may not only be disappointing but could be so alarming that you question the logic of continuing. Indeed, unless you understand the rules of heredity this would seem a sensible conclusion. It is not unknown for a first result to be so catastrophic that the breeder is put off the idea of inbreeding for ever.

However, when used correctly inbreeding is a most valuable asset to serious breeders as it will very quickly reveal all the hidden problems associated with their stock. If faults are continually masked then the breeder is not only unaware of them but unable to take steps to eradicate them. Rigorous selection will allow the breeder eventually to breed stock that is pure in its genetic make-up for the desired characteristics and which will in the future breed true for these characteristics.

If your foundation stock is displaying a serious fault then before contemplating inbreeding you should conduct matings to produce stock that does not display this fault. You must always remember that although the offspring do not display the fault, it is very likely that they may still carry these recessive genes hidden. However, the very fact that they do not display the original fault proves that they must also carry the dominant gene to counteract the fault. From here, by the use of carefully thought-out inbreeding and by rejecting any animal showing this fault, it is possible to produce a strain of animals that breeds true and no longer carries the unwanted gene.

It has been stated many times, even by respected breeders, that inbreeding is responsible for introducing such conditions as impotency, sterility, loss of size, reduced size of litters, aggression, and timidity. However, for these conditions to occur at all the genes responsible for them must already be present in the parents and ancestors; if the defects are not visible then the genes are still present but recessive and hidden. All that inbreeding did in these cases was to make apparent the hidden factors in a breeder's choice of stock.

Line-Breeding

Many breeders who are strongly opposed to inbreeding are avid supporters of line-breeding. The two methods are fairly similar in so far as the animals used are closely related. It is more commonly agreed in line-breeding that while it is unacceptable to mate father to daughter and the like, the mating of uncle to niece and grandfather to granddaughter are within the bounds of acceptability.

The prime objective of line-breeding is to mate together animals that are descended from a selected common ancestor. In this way it is hoped that the common ancestor should play a large part in the genetic make-up of the resultant offspring. With this method it is

Ch. Oldwell Toby of Studbergh.

advantageous if at least two, and possibly three, different matings are arranged using descendants of the same common ancestor. The programme should then be to mate offspring from these unions to the offspring from the earlier union, thus compounding the influence of the common ancestor.

The advantages of this method when compared to inbreeding are that any faults that may occur are less likely to be fixed, although the same applies to the desirable points. Progeny of a similar quality in appearance to those resulting from inbreeding can usually be produced, but because more genetic combinations are possible as a larger number of differently bred animals is used, the genetic possibilities of such dogs breeding true are greatly reduced compared to inbreeding.

The concept of line-breeding is often misunderstood. A breeder may claim that a dog is line-bred to one of his ancestors, whereas in reality he means that one line of the dog's pedigree can be traced directly to one ancestor that appears only once in the pedigree; such a dog cannot truly be considered to be line-bred.

Outcrossing

The term outcrossing is often used to describe the mating of unrelated stock, although when used in this context the definition is

Ch. Copperfield Samson.

technically incorrect. Outcrossing is specifically the mating of a line-bred dog to a dog that is line-bred from a different line, thus the line is outcrossed.

Most breeders have to face the possibility of using an outcross at some time. Because the genetic make-up of an inbred or line-bred dog is fixed, the only possibility left to a breeder who wishes to correct a fault is the outcross, preferably from a line that excels in the point to be corrected. The resultant offspring should then be mated back within the breeder's original strain. That said, if you use an outcross it is important to remember that you should be extremely careful when selecting future breeding stock from such a union. In your quest to improve your stock it is possible that you may breed a dog with many faults that are not apparent in the parents.

Random Breeding

The mating of completely unrelated animals that are themselves the product of such a mating is called random mating and should only be considered as a last resort. While mating your bitch to the latest champion dog may produce an outstanding show specimen, it is equally possible that this latest champion is completely the wrong match for your bitch so that together they produce only mediocre puppies. If the pair does produce a top-quality show specimen then it is quite likely that due to their genetic make-up such progeny will be unable to reproduce dogs of a similar quality. Random breeding is unlikely to fix specific points or characteristics, and does not constitute a serious breeding programme.

The Brood-Bitch

The brood-bitch is the foundation of your kennel, and as such she should be well-bred and free from as many undesirable characteristics as possible. It is imperative that the brood-bitch is sound in temperament, and that she shows no signs of viciousness or timidity; such bitches should not be considered suitable for any breeding programme. She must be a first-class representative of the breed and must be of the correct size. It should be noted that the practice of continually using undersized bitches for breeding purposes will inevitably lead to the lowering of overall height in the breed. Any bitch that is only 20in (50cm) or so tall must give cause for concern.

It is better to have a top-quality bitch with a single highly undesirable fault than a mediocre bitch with many minor faults as it is easier to correct one major fault than to improve overall mediocrity. Although the occasional outstanding specimen may be produced from a poor-quality bitch, it is unlikely that the breeder will be able to repeat such a result. This is even less likely today, when so few breeders keep large numbers of bitches. It cannot therefore be stressed enough that the quality of the breeding bitches in any kennel must be considered of paramount importance.

When deciding on your foundation bitch take note of all her virtues and, even more important, her failings. Study her pedigree carefully; try to estimate from which dogs her virtues came and from which her failings. Remember that the perfect dog has yet to be born, but that your aim should always be to attain such perfection.

Care of the Brood-Bitch

Before breeding, a bitch should be in hard, lean, muscular condition, and should also be both alert and attentive to her surroundings. Overweight bitches tend to have more irregular intervals between seasons and usually conceive less easily than fit bitches. She should be fed a properly balanced diet and exercised regularly as this is beneficial both in carrying the puppies and in the act of giving birth. Exercise tones up all the muscles and ligaments of the body, including those used in helping the womb to contract and thus expel the puppies. It goes without saying that before mating the bitch should have been vaccinated against all the usual diseases, and that she should also have been treated for worms, parasites and the like.

Common sense should always prevail when deciding at what age the bitch should be mated. It is generally accepted in the UK that bitches should not be mated until they are twenty months old, while in some other countries it is considered quite acceptable to mate bitches younger than this. We feel that if you have waited this long then you might as well wait until her next season as this will probably be better for her. After all, it is only a matter of waiting a few extra months, but it could make all the difference to your bitch, her puppies, and any future litters. The act of carrying, whelping, and rearing a litter may cause an immature bitch to suffer from irregular oestrus and hence have problems with future breeding. Consequently, a bitch should not under normal circumstances be bred from until she has attained full maturity. There are, of course, the occasional exceptions to this general rule, but when these do occur a great deal of thought and care should be exercised before you go ahead with the mating.

Oestrus

As a general rule bitches come into season from the age of six months, and from there on at six-monthly intervals. However, it is not uncommon for Bullmastiffs to have their first season as late as twelve or even, on rare occasions, fifteen months of age. Remember that although the bitch is capable of producing puppies at this time she is still physically and mentally very much a baby. The period a bitch is in season usually lasts approximately three weeks. Many breeders have noticed that during an exceptionally cold spell, when conditions would not be ideal for a bitch in the wild to rear a litter, bitches may be delayed coming into season.

The first noticeable sign that a bitch is coming into season is a swelling of the vulva; in the puppy, where the vulva is small, this swelling is even more noticeable. This is followed after a few days by a slightly discoloured discharge, which then turns to pink and eventually red as the old cells of the uterus wall are shed. A new layer of specialized cells then develops in the uterus to receive the fertilized eggs. The discharge is visible as spots of blood down the legs, on the floor, and in the bitch's bed, although with some secretive bitches the only signs you may see are spots of blood on her

Graecia Lancer.

bedding. Any discharge other than that described may be a cause for concern and should be checked with your vet.

It is not uncommon for a bitch to display very few or even none of the outward signs of oestrus, while conversely some bitches have excessive or prolonged bleeding, or may come into season at very short intervals. Any of these conditions could indicate an abnormality or disorder in the reproductive system, and before you consider mating the bitch it would therefore be advisable to discuss the problem with your veterinary surgeon.

As she approaches the time for mating the bitch may begin to flirt with other bitches, mounting them and in turn allowing them to mount her. This is perfectly normal behaviour. By the time she is ready for mating the swelling of the vulva will have subsided and on examination will be found to be soft and pliable. In many cases the bleeding will have decreased to such an extent that there is now only a pale straw-coloured discharge. It is shortly after this that the bitch ovulates and will therefore be receptive.

Ovulation occurs when the eggs, or ova, produced in the ovaries are released. They are carried down the fallopian tubes, where they will meet any sperm that have already made their way through the vagina and uterus. The ova are then fertilized and move down to the horns of the uterus; it is also possible that some of the ova may be fertilized after their arrival in the uterus. The size of the litter sired by a fit, virile dog is only limited by the number of ripe ova present in the oviduct. Mother Nature does, however, tend to be overgenerous, and

147

it is quite normal for more ova to be present and fertilized than the actual number of puppies born.

It is pointless to mate the bitch before ovulation occurs – usually between the tenth and fourteenth days after commencement of the season, although this is only a rough guide and cannot be relied upon. We have experience of bitches ovulating from as early as the third day to as late as the nineteenth day.

There are many ways to determine at what time in her season a bitch should be mated. The most common, and one that has been widely used by experienced breeders for a number of years, is to observe the actions of the bitch as you gently stroke the area near the base of her tail, the back of the hind leg to the side of the vulva, or the area just above the vulva. When ready, a bitch stroked in these areas will generally raise her tail and move it to one side, at the same time raising her vulva as if for presentation to the dog.

A further method, which is a little more scientific, is to have your vet take a swab from as close to the cervix as possible. A slide made using this swab is then examined under a microscope to assess the cells. As the time of ovulation approaches the cell content and structure changes gradually, so that the number of white corpuscles increases while the red corpuscles become fewer and change shape slightly.

An up-to-date method that appears to be increasing in popularity amongst breeders is what is loosely termed as a pre-mate test. A sample of blood is taken, and from this it is possible to determine the exact time of ovulation by detecting the peak rise of luteinizing hormone. In general, the level of luteinizing hormone peaks and then returns to normal within a twenty-four-hour period, and at the same time levels of the hormone progesterone begin to rise. If a surge of luteinizing hormone or a rise in progesterone is detected then it can be assumed that ovulation will usually occur approximately forty-eight hours later. While some breeders believe this is the best time to effect a mating, it is far more advantageous to wait at least a further forty-eight hours to give the ova time to mature so that they are more easily penetrated by the sperm.

Correctly timimg that the mating of bitches has become easier through the use of pre-mate tests as they take all the guesswork out of the mating game: no longer is it a struggle to effect a mating because you do not know whether a bitch is ready or not. When we first used a pre-mate test for one of our bitches we did not take it seriously. The test revealed that she would ovulate two days later, on the fifteenth day of her season. Unfortunately, heavy snowfalls prevented us from taking the bitch to the dog until some four days later, when the bitch was on her nineteenth day (and therefore, according to the test, still receptive). We decided to take a chance and made the journey to the stud-dog. Despite our doubts about her conceiving she later produced an excellent litter. From then on we became firm believers in pre-mate tests, and although we use them only on occasion we have no doubts about recommending them.

The Stud-Dog

The choice of stud-dog is extremely important. First and foremost you should make sure that the dog you intend to use is physically fit, healthy, and free from any infections that could be transmitted to your bitch. Much careful thought should have gone into the selection of a stud-dog long before the bitch is ready for mating. Do not leave the decision until the last few days and then in desperation rush to the nearest and most convenient dog, which might be completely wrong for your bitch.

Ch. Graecia Mercury, Best in Breed at Crufts 1996, and Top Stud-dog (UK) 1997 and 1998.

When selecting a dog it is imperative that you not only assess the physical and mental attributes of the dog himself, but whenever possible pay particular attention to any of his offspring, noting specifically all of their qualities and faults. Any stud-dog is only as good as the quality of the offspring he produces, and the best-looking dog in the world is of little value if he only produces mediocre offspring. Pay special attention to his immediate ancestors and siblings. Does he follow a similar type?

Hopefully you will be able to study the stud-dog's pedigree, not merely as a list of names but through first-hand knowledge of the dogs named therein. If you did not know these dogs personally then make enquiries of people who did as they may be able to furnish you with additional information. The pedigree should extend back at least five generations, and further if possible. For each of the names that appears, again note all known qualities and faults.

Always remember that although the proposed sire may not show a particular fault, he may well carry it in his genetic make-up if one of his parents or grandparents did so. The use of such a dog should certainly be regarded with caution if either of your bitch's parents or grandparents displayed this same fault. In this case, even though neither your bitch nor the prospective sire displays the fault, there is a good chance that a number of their offspring will do so.

No dog, no matter how good he is, can produce outstanding puppies every time; some of the offspring will undoubtedly show undesirable qualities. Make a mental note of the faults and at the same time assess the qualities of the partnering dam. After seeing both parents and their progeny, assess which points the sire may have corrected or otherwise, taking on board the fact that he has only contributed 50 per cent of the genetic make-up of the puppies.

Be very careful when attributing faults to genes as there are a number of faults – for example, poor bones, skeletal disorders, lack of size, bad feet, cow hocks, or poor temperament that can be put down to environmental factors or inexperienced rearing. Poor nutrition, failure to socialize puppies, lack of exercise, and general bad stockmanship can also on occasion be responsible for all of these conditions. If such characteristics are apparent in the offspring, you must ascertain whether they are a result of environmental influences or the dog's genetic make-up before you decide if the sire is a suitable stud-dog for your bitch.

Try to establish whether or not the stud-dog is prepotent for the desired breed characteristics. It is at least as important, if not more so, to determine which characteristics are carried hidden in his genetic make-up. In the main, the offspring of a prepotent sire will resemble such a sire in all aspects, both desirable and undesirable. The closer the stud-dog resembles his family line the more likely he will be to produce a similar type of offspring. However, if he is the product of a random mating he will be less likely to reproduce his own likeness even though he may be an exceptionally good-looking dog.

Under no circumstances should you select a dog that displays faults similar to those of your bitch, regardless of how good he appears or how many wins he has achieved. Such a mating will inevitably be detrimental to your future stock.

Care of the Stud-Dog

The care of a stud-dog is of paramount importance if you want him to be healthy, virile, and capable of performing his duties in a satisfactory manner to a reasonable age. He must not only be an excellent representative of the breed, but must also be kept in tip-top condition so that he is sound in mind, wind, and limb. Like a thoroughbred horse he must command the admiration of all. We have found that it is extremely beneficial to start when the dog is aged between ten and twelve months, especially with a matron bitch who will encourage him, and then to leave him until he is at least eighteen months old. By introducing him to the mating game at such an early age he will soon learn what is expected of him and should never have problems in the future. At this age he is also more inclined to allow you to help him, and so in the future will always be happy to accept this help.

With regards feeding, the stud-dog must be provided with a wholesome diet containing adequate levels of protein and minerals and vitamins, particularly vitamins E and B complex. This can either be achieved using a modern complete feed, manufactured for the purpose, or a varied and balanced home-constituted diet containing quantities of raw meat, fish, milk, eggs, fruit, and vegetables. Whichever method is used, the dog must be fed sufficient to keep him in a lean, hard, muscular condition, whereby you can feel his ribs but cannot see them when standing back from the dog. Obesity can be extremely detrimental to a stud-dog and his performance, and should always be avoided.

The dog should receive regular exercise, and should not only be walked on a lead but also allowed to run free. The amount of exercise should be geared to keeping him in a hard, muscular condition, for it is no use feeding to build muscle if that muscle volume is then allowed to decrease due to lack of exercise.

It goes without saying that he should be kept up to date with all vaccinations and boosters. (It is now also becoming quite common for stud-dog owners in the UK to ask that visiting bitches are examined by a vet prior to the visit, and then a certificate issued to confirm that she is healthy and free from disease and parasites.)

After serving each bitch, and more often if necessary, the stud-dog's genital organs should be examined as it is possible he may suffer injury in the course of mating. Small blood vessels in the penis may rupture and cause bleeding, which can be cause for concern. It is not unusual for a dog to have a slight discharge from the prepuce; this should be checked periodically, and if necessary the area should be cleaned and your vet consulted.

Other than the bitches he is to serve, the stud-dog should have no contact with any other bitch in the kennel that comes into season. If he does so he may fret, become frustrated, and refuse to eat, and as a result may then lose condition. These reasons aside, it would in any case be unfair to the dog.

Before considering any mating it is advisable for stud-dog owners to check the pedigree and registration certificates of the bitch to verify that she is registered with The Kennel Club in the correct name of

Austral. Ch. Weilhana Lord Brutus, Bullmastiff of the Year (South Australia) from 1991 to 1994.

the owner. Finally, before agreeing to allow a stud-dog to mate any bitch, all stud-dog owners should satisfy themselves that the bitch is of sufficient quality to warrant mating. You will do the breed in general and your dog in particular no favours if you allow a mating of an inferior-quality bitch.

The Mating

Although there is nothing more natural than the act of mating, man's desire to breed from selected dogs has increased the likelihood that problems will occur.

It is the usual practice for the bitch to be taken to the dog. Before the bitch is introduced to the dog you should examine her. First, ensure that there is no vaginal discharge other than that normally associated with her season. There must be no strictures and her vulva must be soft and relaxed. If a small stricture is suspected, experienced breeders will in most cases be able to deal with it; otherwise you should consult your vet.

If possible, put the dog and bitch side by side in separate pens when they meet for the first time, then if they show a keen interest in each other introduce them while keeping them on leads and under complete control (we advocate a second, strong leather collar for the bitch). If the bitch is definitely ready then there should be no problems, but it is wise to be prepared for any eventuality, especially if she is a young maiden bitch.

Some stud-dogs will quite often play with the bitch, but only if the bitch wants to do so. If she appears frightened or distraught by this behaviour then give her more time until she is happy about the dog's advances. The performance of courtship is a natural opening move to the act of mating and the bitch should be given every chance to become accustomed to the dog's advances. A bitch that is being restrained can become bewildered and panic-stricken, and will then do everything in her power to resist. Be patient and allow time for the dog and bitch to settle down and get to know each other so that they can complete in their own time what is after all perfectly natural. If a bitch is so stressed by the idea of mating then she is either not ready, is physically immature, or is just not adjusted mentally to accept the act of mating at this time. If a bitch is determined that she has no desire whatsoever to be mated then it is best to respect her wishes. Quite often at her next season she will be quite happy to be mated without any fuss.

Providing everything is under control and the bitch is definitely receptive, let the pair get on with it by themselves, although you should hold the bitch's head in case of any mishaps. When the bitch permits the dog to mount he will naturally try to find the entrance to the vulva with his penis. An inexperienced dog may need your assistance in this, or if he has trouble effecting penetration apply a little petroleum jelly or KY gel to the vulva. Once he has penetrated the vulva he will give a series of strong thrusting movements. The base of the penis will then expand and he will ejaculate. At approximately the same time the constrictor muscle of the vulva will contract, effectively gripping the dog's penis behind the posterior gland to form the tie. Although the tie is considered by many to be evidence of a successful mating, it is not necessary – and conception can and does occur without it.

Although most bitches will stand still after the initial few minutes, some may become excited or fearful at this stage and try to pull away from the dog; if this is the case the person handling the bitch should hold her steady and give her encouragement. After ejaculation the dog will grasp the bitch securely and remain on her back until the tie is secured. He should then be allowed to dismount to one side of the bitch, and the handler should gently lift his rear leg over the bitch so that they are back to back. It is also common for a stud-dog to be allowed to dismount and stand alongside the bitch.

If both dog and bitch are perfectly happy with this, then it is just a matter of staying there to steady them. If, on the other hand, the bitch is excitable and venomously resents the mating, then not only will one handler be required to control the bitch's head but a second handler will also be needed to make sure that she does not attempt to sit down or try to pull away from the dog, and possibly a third handler to steady the dog. If you suspect that the bitch will behave in this manner it is advisable to muzzle the bitch. However, if you are patient it should be possible to effect a mating without resorting to such methods, and it is only on very rare occasions that three handlers will be necessary.

Stud Fee

The stud fee, which will have been agreed beforehand, should normally be paid to the owner of the sire after the completion of the mating. This agreed fee covers the services of the stud-dog and

Northern Light of Evenstar.

nothing else. However, if the bitch does not conceive most reputable owners of stud-dogs will agree to a free mating at the bitch's next season, providing the dog is still available. The bitch's owner has no right to expect or demand this, and it is only granted with the goodwill of the stud-dog's owner.

There is a misconception amongst many owners of bitches that paying a stud fee guarantees puppies; this is definitely not so. There are many reasons why a bitch does not conceive, the most obvious of which is that she was mated at the wrong time in her cycle. Determining when a bitch is most likely to conceive is the responsibility of her owner, who cannot expect the stud-dog owner continually to allow use of his dog free of charge. By serving the bitch the stud-dog has fulfilled his side of the agreement.

To avoid any misunderstandings some owners of stud-dogs adopt a policy whereby they allow the owner of the bitch to choose whether to pay the stud fee at the time of mating or when he or she is certain the bitch is in whelp. This system is often better for both parties. The stud-dog owner will usually allow a free repeat mating at a convenient time if the bitch does not conceive at first attempt.

No matter what the agreement, it is essential to finalize all aspects before the actual mating. If, for example, the stud-dog owner is to have his pick of the litter, then you must decide in advance what will happen if there is only one live puppy. By discussing all the eventualities you will eliminate the possibility of any misunderstandings and resultant unpleasantness later on. If you are in any doubt, put the terms in writing so that each party is fully aware of what is expected.

Infertility

It is generally accepted that if live, virile sperm meet the ripe ova in the fallopian tubes the result will be puppies. As breeders we are all too aware that this is not always the case. There are many and varied reasons why puppies are not born, the most common of which would appear to be timing. No matter how often a bitch is mated, if she has not ovulated by the time the sperm reach the fallopian tubes then no ova will be present to fertilize. The same applies if she is mated too late in her cycle, when all the ova will have been released and passed out of the bitch's body. Even with the knowledge available today many breeders continue to insist that a bitch should be mated on a specific day of her season as opposed to when ovulation has actually occurred.

Infections of the uterus or vagina are often reasons for infertility in bitches. The most common of these is metritis, which is an infection of the lining of the uterus. It is more usual for this to occur after whelping, when the infection can affect future fertility or, in the worst case, develop into pyometra (see Chapter 10).

Causes for sterility in a stud-dog can be attributed to his overuse. If an outstanding dog is in great demand for stud work then the owner should think seriously about the frequency at which he is used. Unfortunately, some stud-dog owners find it hard to refuse a request for stud. Lack of exercise is a further consideration. Exercise tones up every part of the body, and it has been found that dogs given regular daily exercise are more fertile than those receiving little or no exercise. Diet also plays an extremely important part in fertility. It is

Ch. Naukeen Lorraine.

essential that both the dog and bitch receive a well-balanced diet, in particular containing adequate levels of vitamin E.

Finally, it is possible that the sperm could be deficient. If a sperm has no tail or if its tail is bent or damaged then it will not be able to travel through the uterus to the fallopian tubes. Further possible problems are that the head of the sperm is unable to penetrate the ova, or that the sperm itself is dead. Your veterinary surgeon will be able to confirm most of these conditions by examining the sperm under the microscope.

9

Pregnancy and Whelping

Signs of Pregnancy

Once your bitch has been mated you will now have to wait and see if she is pregnant. Every breeder seems to have his or her own method by which to confirm pregnancy, but if for any reason it is imperative that you know then one of the more positive ways of confirming it is to ask your vet to palpate the bitch's abdomen in the hope of locating the foetuses, which at this stage can best be described as resembling a string of pearls. The best time to perform this is between the twentieth and twenty-fifth days after mating. However, palpitation methods must be left to those who are experienced as it is possible to damage the unborn foetus.

Another method that is becoming more popular is the ultrasound scan. Again, use professional people with the sound knowledge of the procedure. A third way is simply to wait for the tell-tale signs. From the fourth week the teats may become larger and go pink at the tips, the vulva will often remain soft and pliable, and may not return to its normal state, the bitch's waistline will thicken slightly, and she will tend to display slight changes in her normal behaviour pattern.

From six weeks onwards her teats will become more enlarged and there will be a definite increase in her girth caused by the growth of the foetus, and by the placentas and extra fluid she is carrying. After the sixth week, in a normal-sized litter you should be able to see the puppies moving whilst the bitch is resting, especially if she is sleeping and relaxed.

False Pregnancy

It sometimes happens that a bitch experiences a false or phantom pregnancy. In the vast majority of these cases the bitch will display all the normal symptoms associated with pregnancy, even to the extent of producing milk and going through the usual ritual of nesting. Some days later she may then take any objects she fancies into the nest and treat them as puppies. This behaviour may last for a week or two, after which the bitch will revert to her normal self.

Care of the Pregnant Bitch

Don't make the common mistake of overfeeding the pregnant bitch in the first four to five weeks in the false hope that by doing so you will give her whelps a good start. All you will achieve is an overweight brood who, because of obesity, may then have difficulties delivering her puppies. Instead, feed her normal daily amounts, if necessary increasing the number of feeds.

From six weeks onwards you should begin to increase the quantities, especially of high-quality foods. It is of far less value to increase the carbohydrates than it is to feed high-quality foods based on animal proteins. If the bitch is not fed with such high-quality foods she will have no way of passing on the nutrients, vitamins, and minerals required by her whelps. Remember also that a pregnant bitch's fluid requirements are far greater than normal, so always make fresh drinking water available.

In the later weeks of pregnancy you must take care with her exercise; no longer should she be allowed to gallop about with the other dogs, and obviously playing rough games with them or with members of your family must cease. However, do not be tempted to wrap her in cotton wool and ensure that she has adequate exercise – a pregnant bitch is not an invalid, but nevertheless she should not be allowed to become overtired.

Occasionally during pregnancy a bitch may have a vaginal discharge. As long as this is only slight, and is colourless and odourless, there is no need for undue concern. However, if there is a lot of discharge or if it is dark in colour – for example, yellow or green – either whelping is imminent or there may be a problem, such as an infection of the vagina or uterus. If you are in any doubt whatsoever consult your veterinary surgeon, for it is wiser to be safe than sorry.

Very rarely a bitch may miscarry or abort. When this does happen the probable causes are ill health, injury, trauma, violence, or abnormality of the whelps or the bitch's reproductive system. Always take special care to avoid any sudden upsets or shocks, such as fireworks or any other loud bangs. If she is frightened of thunder then a word with your veterinary surgeon may be in order.

Preparation for Whelping

Do not leave it until the last minute to introduce your bitch to her expected whelping quarters. Instead, show her the whelping box at least two weeks before she is due to whelp, put her bedding into the box, and encourage her to sleep in it. In this way she will accept it as hers.

The whelping quarters should be light, airy, warm, and well ventilated with a free flow of fresh air. We recommend a wooden whelping box measuring approximately 48in deep by 54in wide by 22 in high (122 × 137 × 56cm). Although it is possible to buy fibreglass or plastic whelping boxes, a home-made wooden one has the advantage that it can easily be repaired if it is damaged through chewing. The base of a DIY box should be constructed from lengths of 2 × 2in (5 × 5cm) wood, onto which you fit a sheet of plywood 1in (2.5cm) thick. The four sides are again made from plywood 1in (2.5cm) thick, and each corner is supported by a piece of 2 × 2in (5 × 5cm) wood sawn in half diagonally; this will ensure that there are no sharp edges to the corners of the box. A section measuring 30 ×

Austral. Ch. Little Treasure of Graecia, four weeks in whelp.

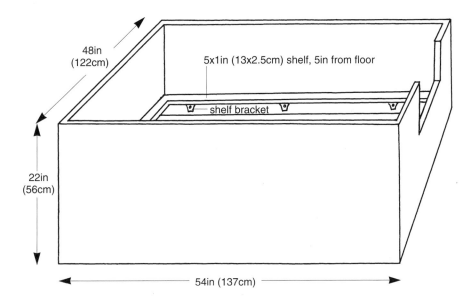

Recommended dimensions of a whelptng box.

12in (76 × 30cm) is then cut out of one end of the box, and on either side of the created gap a piece of 1½ × ½in (4 × 1.3cm) wood is fitted. This will form guides into which the previously removed section can be slipped. Rails made from 5 × 1in (13 × 2.5cm) timber are fitted into the box and secured to it 5in (13cm) from the floor with shelf brackets. (We have found that these rails help protect any puppy that may get trapped behind the bitch.) When the construction of the box is completed, apply two coats of yacht varnish to allow easy cleaning.

As your bitch's due date approaches, you should collect together everything you may need for the whelping. This should include a sharp pair of sterilized round-ended scissors, a pair of artery forceps, and a few lengths of surgical thread (cat gut), all of which should have been soaked in a mild solution of good-quality antiseptic (they may be required on the very rare occasions that it is necessary to tie the umbilical cord). You should also have lots of large, clean towels (to be used for drying the puppies on delivery), plenty of clean newspaper, a bottle of antiseptic, and small squares of clean towelling (for grasping slippery puppies to aid their birth). It is a sound idea to instal an infrared lamp over and to one side of the whelping box.

Ch. Naukeen Angela.

The Birth

The textbook pregnancy is supposed to last for sixty-three days, but don't expect this to be the case with every pregnancy. Depending on how large and heavily in whelp the bitch is, she may whelp anytime between the fifty-seventh and sixty-ninth days. If a bitch is very heavy in whelp then be prepared for the fact that she might naturally go into premature labour. Providing this is not too early in the pregnancy (before the fifty-sixth day), and as long as the newborn puppies are kept warm and dry, it should not be cause for concern and the puppies will have a good chance of survival. That said, it is possible that a bitch whelping this early may not have sufficient milk

162

to feed her puppies, so to be on the safe side have some puppy-rearing milk on hand plus a feeding bottle (*see* Hand-Rearing).

Just as it is perfectly acceptable for a bitch to whelp early, it is quite possible for her to go past the day on which she is due to whelp. There should be no cause for concern if she is up to two days late, unless she or her pups are showing signs of distress. It is always a wise precaution after two days to have her examined by your veterinary surgeon to confirm everything is normal.

Some of the early signs that whelping is imminent are that the bitch goes off her food some twenty-four to forty-eight hours beforehand. At the same time she may appear to be unsettled, wandering about, and her temperature may drop from the normal 101.5°F (38.6°C) to approximately 99°F (37.2°C); we have even known it to drop as low as 97°F (36.1°C). She may start nesting, scratching up carpets and rugs, or even ripping her own bedding.

The first stage of labour sees the body of the uterus, vagina, and vulva relaxing and then dilating in preparation for the passage of the puppies down the birth canal. The vagina will begin to soften, and at about the same time the bitch may have a 'show', whereby the thick transparent or slightly opaque mucous-like discharge that forms the cervical plug comes away. As this first stage of labour progresses she may begin to shiver slightly, usually along the length of her back and occasionally down her sides. These shivers tend to manifest themselves as ripples, similar to those seen on water. The first stage usually lasts twenty-four to forty-eight hours, although it can go on for anything up to five days. If it continues for more than two days it is advisable to consult your veterinary surgeon as she may be suffering from uterine inertia (*see* below).

During the second stage of labour the shivers will give way to strong rhythmical contractions as the muscles of the uterus tighten. As time goes by these contractions will increase in frequency. The bitch will appear to hold her breath and tense or arch her body during each contraction, and then pant as the uterus relaxes. If this is her first confinement she will need all of the encouragement and reassurance you can give.

If all goes well then the sac of the first puppy should present itself fairly soon, and with the next one or two contractions the puppy should be born. Puppies usually come head first, although it is not uncommon for them to be presented hind legs first in what is known as posterior presentation.

When the puppy is finally born let the bitch clear the sac from him and bite through the umbilical cord. It is quite normal for a bitch to eat the entire membranous sac and the placenta, and although you may find this offensive you should not stop her from doing so. The placenta is not only high in nutritional value but also contains a substance that helps bring on the bitch's milk. If she does eat the placenta her motions for the next few days may be loose and black in colour, but this is nothing to worry about. Next, let her lick and clean the puppy as this action will help to stimulate the puppy's circulation and breathing.

Never, without good reason, discourage the bitch from behaving naturally. If for any reason the bitch cannot or will not perform these tasks, then you must do so. Remove the sac from the puppy's head and mouth to enable him to draw his first breath. As long as the puppy's head is cleared of the sac so that he can breathe, then it is not necessary to sever the cord immediately. Instead, it is better to delay this for a minute or two to allow the transfer of blood between the placenta and puppy to decrease.

When it does come to cutting the cord, lay the puppy on the floor of the whelping box, support him with one hand, and use your round-ended scissors to cut the cord approximately 2–3in (5–8cm) from the puppy's navel. Do not allow the weight of the placenta to pull on the puppy as this may cause an umbilical hernia. If the cord continues to bleed, tie off the end using a length of thread. You may find it better to sever the cord using your thumbnail as this method not only compresses the cord during separation but does not leave as sharp a cut as that left by scissors, and will therefore not bleed as much. To discourage bleeding it is always advisable to run the cord between your finger and thumb in the direction of the puppy before cutting it.

After severing the cord pick the puppy up between two hands and rub him vigorously with a clean towel. This not only dries the puppy, but the action of rubbing will stimulate the circulation and encourage him to breathe and clear his lungs.

Some breeders remove each puppy immediately after birth and put it in a box into which has been placed a hot-water bottle wrapped in a towel. The idea behind this is that the puppies will be safer away from the bitch whilst she is giving birth to the later arrivals. However, we believe that it is better to leave the puppies with the bitch as otherwise she may suffer distress. In any case, it is beneficial to allow the puppies to suckle in between each delivery. This not only encourages the milk to flow, but also stimulates the release of hormones from the pituitary gland into the bloodstream that in turn stimulate the muscles of the uterus to contract. The milk produced during these early feeds and for the first three or four days after birth is called colostrum, and is rich in antibodies. The transfer of these antibodies from the dam to the puppies will protect them and see them safely through the first few weeks of life.

The intervals between the birth of each of the puppies can vary from as little as ten minutes to a couple of hours, although one may be born immediately after the previous one. After the bitch has given birth to a number of puppies the contractions may cease. During this time, which may last from an hour upwards, the bitch may sleep while the puppies suckle happily. This rest period is extremely beneficial in that it allows the bitch to recuperate before contractions to produce more puppies resume.

Accompanying the birth of each puppy should be the placenta, attached to the puppy via the umbilical cord. It is essential that all the placentas are passed as any that are retained may subsequently decompose to form a serious infection inside the bitch. Keep a count of all the placentas, and if at the completion of the birth you are unsure whether any have been retained then consult your vet who will probably administer oxytocin to the bitch. This will cause the uterus to contract and so expel any remaining matter.

Ch. Hooksdean Tinkabell of Liccassa.

Whelping Complications

Obstruction

Despite strong contractions a bitch may occasionally fail to deliver a puppy. The cause may be inertia (*see* next page), but it may also be that the puppy is very large or is presenting itself incorrectly and is therefore unable to progress down the birth canal. Do not let a bitch try to deliver a puppy without success for too long as continual strong contractions will soon tire her to the point of exhaustion. Should she then need a general anaesthetic for a caesarean section the risk to her would be that much greater.

On examination it is sometimes found that although the puppy is presenting normally at the pelvis the bitch has difficulty in moving him forward. In such a case slide your fingers to either side of the puppy and hold him so that you are able to stop him from sliding back. With each contraction the puppy should then advance slightly, so that if you manage to hold him in position he will be born after the next contraction or two. *Never pull the puppy.* Instead, wait for the contractions and support these. Before any such examination, make sure your hands are scrupulously clean and well lubricated, paying particular attention to your fingernails which should be short, smooth, and scrubbed clean.

Puppies are usually presented for birth head first, although it is also common for them to be presented rear end first. While there should be no great difficulties with either of these presentations, there are occasions when puppies present with the head bent down to the chest, the head bent backwards, the limbs placed incorrectly, or the body positioned transversely to the pelvis. In some cases it will be necessary to perform a caesarean section, but in most others the experienced breeder can carefully manipulate the puppies into the correct position. If you have any doubts whatsoever it is always advisable to consult your veterinary surgeon.

We cannot stress enough here that the above methods of assistance should only be employed in an emergency situation. You should always be aware of the possible dangers associated with any untrained physical interference, in particular damage to the delicate membranes of the bitch and the chance of introducing infection (which can have very serious consequences). We would advise that unless you are absolutely certain of what you are doing you should always obtain professional veterinary assistance.

Inertia

There are commonly two reasons for this condition. The first occurs when the puppy is either extra large, has a large skull, or is presented in such a way as to make it difficult, if not impossible, to be delivered normally. After a long period of strong contractions the muscles of the uterus will become exhausted, and then lose their ability to contract and thus expel the puppy. The common course of action in such a case is to perform a caesarean section, hopefully before the bitch becomes too exhausted.

The second type of inertia is characterized by the bitch's failure to begin contractions after the first stage of labor. It is thought to be hereditary and is usually the result of a hormonal imbalance. Other possible reasons are that the bitch is in poor condition, possibly brought about by a lack of exercise or incorrect nutrition, that she is too old to be used for breeding, or that her pregnancies have been too frequent. This type of inertia can quite often be redressed in the early stages by injecting a calcium solution, which gently stimulates the contractions.

The most serious effects of inertia are first that the delay in the birth of the puppy will cause problems for the bitch and may result in the deaths of any unborn puppies. The second danger is that the lack of muscular contractions may cause the uterus wall to bleed for longer than is usual after the separation of the placenta.

A more powerful drug administered by the veterinary surgeon to bring on contractions is oxytocin, a hormone produced naturally by the pituitary gland. Great care should be taken when administering this drug to ensure that there are no obstructions in the birth canal and that the cervix is completely dilated. If used correctly oxytocin should produce results within a period of five to twenty minutes. If it does not work within half an hour then it may be administered once more, but if it fails again a caesarean section must be considered.

Caesarean Section

Should your veterinary surgeon decide that the only course of action left open to him is to perform a caesarean section, there is no need for undue worry. Although this is still considered a major operation it should no longer be feared as tremendous advances have been made in anaesthetics and in operation procedures. If it is performed at the correct time the survival rates of both the bitch and puppies are very high. However, if it is performed too early, before the bitch is ready to deliver, then it may be difficult to stem bleeding if the placenta has not separated fully from the wall of the uterus.

During the operation an incision is made along the dorsal aspect of the abdomen (between the two rows of teats), then another is made into the uterus in one or several sites depending on the placement of the puppies. The puppies are removed and then closure commences. All sites on the uterus are sutured, then the abdomen muscle and skin are sutured to leave a surgical wound.

It is possible that on recovering from the anaesthetic the bitch may not want to accept the puppies at all. You must keep a very careful watch on her at this stage, as if she is still slightly disorientated due to the influence of the anaesthetic she may lie on a puppy without realizing he is there. It is also not unknown in this situation for a young bitch, particularly a maiden, to actually attack the puppies. If she does reject the puppies, keep them warm and dry, and if necessary feed them. Give her time to adjust to the idea; her strong maternal instincts will soon be aroused and she should cope perfectly well.

Although she has a large wound she will usually take to the puppies and feeding should continue as normal. Attend to her wound regularly throughout the day, making sure that it is kept clean and dry, especially if a lateral incision was made between the teats.

Resuscitation

Occasionally a puppy will not breathe once he is born. The numerous reasons for this include suffocation caused by the inhalation of fluid in the case of a breech birth, or by excessive pressure during the birth. A long, drawn-out birth may also lead to oxygen starvation after the placenta has separated. There are, however, many ways in which you may be able to revive such a puppy, depending on the length of time that he appears not to have been breathing.

First examine the puppy closely to make sure that his mouth is free of obstruction and that it is not blocked by membranes or mucus. Next, check the colour of the tongue and mouth. If the tongue is white and dry don't expect too much, as nine times out of ten this puppy will have been starved of oxygen for too long. If you do manage to revive such a puppy the probability that he will suffer brain damage is quite high. If, however, the tongue and mouth are still pink then it is possible that you may be able to get this puppy breathing if you act quickly.

Ch. Morejoy Eastern Princess.

Providing there is no fluid coming from the puppy's nose or mouth, take a towel and rub him quite vigorously with it, making sure you hold him head down. By doing so any mucus or fluids that may still be lurking inside the puppy should be pushed out. After you have encouraged the puppy to inflate his lungs – usually accompanied by a squeal – carry on rubbing until he begins to show more signs of life. You can also stimulate the puppy's circulation by placing him alternately in warm and cold water.

A good method by which to expel fluid from the lungs and bronchial and nasal passages is to hold the puppy in both hands with his head and neck well supported by your fingers. Raise the puppy above your head and then bring him down swiftly. Repeat this action a couple of times and then rub the puppy vigorously again. If he shows signs of life then place a spot of brandy on his tongue to encourage him to breathe.

If you need to blow air into the puppy's lungs, do so very gently using the sterilized outer casing of a biro pen (the type with a hole in the side). Use the hole in the casing as a valve, placing a finger over it to control the flow of air. Care should be taken when inserting the casing into the puppy's trachea to ensure that you don't push it too far down or in the wrong place.

Any puppy that has been resuscitated should be kept warm and dry, and allowed to recover away from his litter-mates until he is strong enough to rejoin them.

Post-Whelping Care

A bitch will sometimes lose her appetite for a few days immediately after the birth, but during this time she will still require large quantities of fluid. These fluids can be given in the form of water, milk, sweet tea, or any other drink she fancies. When her appetite does return feed sufficient quantities of high-quality foods. Remember that if you look after the bitch correctly, then she in turn will do an admirable job of rearing the puppies.

Whilst the puppies are suckling it is advisable to keep their claws short at all times, as sharp little claws can seriously hurt and damage a bitch's teats. The bitch should have an adequate supply of all the necessary vitamins and minerals, and if these cannot be supplied by her food then they should be given as a form of supplement. Pay particular attention to any drugs that need to be administered to the bitch, and wherever possible use only natural substances. Unfortunately, many substances administered to the bitch can be transmitted through her milk to the puppies, sometimes with disastrous results.

The temperature of most bitches will rise after the birth, but it should return to normal within forty-eight hours. She will have a bloodstained discharge which should die down gradually until it ceases altogether after a couple of weeks, although it is not uncommon to see the odd spot for a further two weeks. If the discharge should become offensive in any way then seek veterinary assistance as soon as possible.

Make sure that the bitch and her puppies are kept warm, dry, and comfortable. The puppies have no control over their body temperatures until they are approximately three weeks of age, so it is essential to control the ambient temperature. This can best be done by the use of a heat pad, infrared lamp, or, in a specialized whelping room, as a form of space heating.

After the bitch has fulfilled her role and weaning is over, the daily routine of feeding and cleaning rests with you. While the whelping box still serves as the puppies' bed, the whelping quarters now need to act as a den and play area. The area must be secure, with an extension of mesh panels around the whelping box that is high enough to prevent escape but low enough for you to step over. The play area should be spread liberally with newspapers or wood shavings, and the bigger it is the better.

If possible give the puppies a kennel and enclosed pen outside (with, if necessary, a heat lamp over their bed). This is far more beneficial than leaving them inside as they will get plenty of fresh air, while exposure to the sun will allow their bodies to manufacture vitamin D. When they are outside they also seem to grow much quicker and form their own individual characters sooner. If you can, leave their kennel door open all the time to encourage them to venture out into their pen to relieve themselves. To keep the play area dry you could build a temporary lightweight roof, but don't wrap the puppies in cotton wool as they need to acclimatize to the great outdoors as soon as they are able.

Post-Whelping Complications

Eclampsia

Eclampsia, or lactational tetany (also commonly called milk fever), can occur during the later stages of pregnancy or within the first couple of days after whelping, but is more common in the third or fourth week after whelping. The initial symptoms are that the bitch shows signs of becoming excitable and unable to settle. The pupils of the eyes become dilated and she will stare about her as if frightened, with a glazed expression. There may be excessive panting, and she will tend to stagger about with a loss of balance until eventually she collapses. During this time she will have a fast but weak pulse, her temperature may drop significantly, and in severe cases she may suffer convulsions and be frothing at the mouth. In the later stages her body and limbs may become rigid and, if she is not treated quickly, death can occur soon after.

The exact causes of eclampsia are still not known. The condition is generally attributed to a drop in blood calcium levels, and it has been suggested that the activity of the pituitary glands in secreting hormones can upset the delicate balance of the calcium-regulatory mechanism during pregnancy and post whelping. It is interesting to note that eclampsia is much rarer in bitches that are in hard muscular condition and that take regular exercise. More susceptible dogs tend to be overfed and underexercised.

171

Ch. Jagopeeko Boadicea.

The usual treatment is an intravenous or subcutaneous injection of a calcium solution. If treatment is applied in the early stages an almost miraculous and instant recovery is likely. If it is administered in the later stages the success rate is still very good, although recovery may take slightly longer. It is not recommended that you return the bitch to her puppies after treatment, but instead either wean them off as soon as possible or, if necessary, hand-feed them. Only in extreme cases should you consider putting them back with the bitch.

Mastitis

There are several causes of mastitis, and although it has been suggested that it is more prevalent with smaller litters it can in fact occur in litters of any size. The condition occurs when milk is not stripped

172

from a particular teat by the puppies, and instead accumulates there. The teats can then become harder and inflamed.

There are three main stages in the development of mastitis, the first being confined primarily to one teat. The first signs are discoloured milk and hardened areas within the mass of the teat. At this stage the teats should be massaged and bathed with warm water to encourage the milk to start flowing again. If this does not cause the flow to recommence, then bathe the teats alternately in warmer water and then cold; if after a further twenty minutes the milk flow has still not restarted then seek veterinary help. If treated early enough most of these cases can be alleviated successfully with antibiotics.

If the milk is left to collect in one place it can form an ideal culture medium for bacteria. The result is the second stage, namely the development of an abscess. The bitch will usually run a high temperature, and will refuse to eat and to feed her puppies. Veterinary assistance is essential at this stage, and will usually involve the abscess being lanced. Once the infected material has been released the bitch will feel a lot happier, although the teats and the site of the abscess should be gently bathed regularly in order to remove any residue.

If an abscess is left unattended for any length of time the flow of blood to the mammary glands can be affected, and a form of gangrene can occur – this is the third and most serious stage. The first signs can usually be observed as bruising or a dark discoloration in the immediate area of the teats spreading upwards. Although it is uncommon for mastitis to reach this stage, if left untreated it can cause the death of the bitch within two days. The symptoms to be aware of are depression, loss of appetite, high temperature, excessive thirst, and a swelling of the teats together with a bloody discharge. Even though only one or two teats may be involved the symptoms develop at frightening speed and the bitch's condition is extremely serious. Although the condition can be treated successfully with antibiotics and, possibly, surgery, it may result in death if not caught early enough.

Mastitis can result in the loss of some mammary glands and the loss of milk production. It should also be noted that once a bitch has suffered from mastitis the chances of it recurring during future pregnancies are very high.

Fading Puppy Syndrome

Fading puppy syndrome, now believed to be caused by the hepatitis virus, is very distressing for the owner. For the first few days after birth the puppies seem very contented. Their dam pays them all a lot of attention, but then for no apparent reason she starts pushing a certain puppy away to the perimeter of the nest. Despite your attempts to put him back, the dam will keep pushing him away. Not surprisingly, before very long this puppy will begin to wail. Puppies will only cry if they are in pain, or are hungry, cold, or hot. The dam looks and watches this puppy for quite a long time, often crying and whimpering for him, but still not wanting him close to her. If you hold the puppy to his mother's teat in the hope that he may feed, he will not have the strength or the inclination to do so but will still continue to wail.

On examination, the puppy will be colder to the touch than the others in the litter. He will have a sour vinegary smell, and as the hours go by he will become quieter and quieter. The bitch will still insist that she does not wish the puppy to be in the nest with the rest of the litter and will on occasion try to cover him up with the bedding. At this time leave her alone, as she knows best. Eventually, if left, this puppy will die, but before this happens take him away from the dam. A second or even third puppy may begin to wail and show the same symptoms; if this happens you must seek expert veterinary attention immediately.

Puppies with fading puppy syndrome have been saved by the use of subcutaneous injections of glucose, saline, and penicillin solutions. It is advisable to stop the puppies feeding from the bitch as she may be a source of infection.

Hand-Rearing

While there is nothing better for puppies than the bitch's own milk, if she produces very little or none at all then you must resort to a foster mother if one is available, or, failing this, you must bottle-feed the litter yourself. This is quite time-consuming but the end results are worth while and most satisfying.

To hand-feed you will need an 8oz (225ml) baby's feeding bottle together with a couple of anti-colic teats. Any high-quality dried specialized puppy-rearing milk is ideal for feeding newborn puppies. Always mix the milk to the manufacturer's instructions and feed following the recommendations. For the first week the feeds should be given approximately every two hours. Sometimes the puppies may take less, whilst on other occasions they may take a little more. Never underfeed puppies; we find that they usually need to take small

Ch. Celeste of Graecia, top Bullmastiff bitch 1986, a daughter of Ch. Graecia Centaur.

amounts very frequently, just as they would if feeding from their mother.

A faster and more convenient method is to tube-feed the puppies, although problems can be brought on if the feeding is too fast. To use this method, make a mark on the tube equivalent to the distance between the puppy's nose and his last rib. Extend the puppy's head forward and insert the tube down his trachea, keeping to the left-hand side of the throat and taking great care not to feed it into the lungs. If there is any resistance or coughing, remove the tube immediately. Using a syringe, send the milk down the tube and into the stomach, feeding small amounts at a time. Again, if there is any resistance or if the milk comes back up through the puppy's nose, stop and remove the tube immediately. With practice you can become very efficient at this, and will be able to feed a whole litter in a matter of minutes.

If the bitch is still inclined to clean the hand-fed puppies then let her do so; similarly, if she still wishes to cuddle them then let her do so as it will maker her happy, the puppies happy, and in turn you happy! However, if she wants them but refuses to clean them then you will have to do this yourself. Arm yourself with a roll of soft tissue and a sense of humour – it is an extremely time-consuming process to clean puppies. Massage their rectums in order to encourage them to empty their bowels, and then gently rub their genitals to encourage them to empty their bladders. For the first three weeks this procedure must be carried out several times each day. If possible, once you have completed the job give the puppies back to the waiting dam, who no doubt will inspect them to make sure you have done the job properly.

Weaning

Weaning is much easier than it ever used to be. Pet-food manufacturers now prepare special food for just this purpose, and so these foods remove all the guesswork out of trying to ensure that the puppies receive adequate nourishing feeds. That said, we must admit that we still prefer to feed the old-fashioned way. To us it seems a pity to feed the puppies a bland food when with a little time and effort you can achieve the same results while allowing the puppies to become accustomed to many different tastes.

The method we have employed for a number of years is to start with minced beef or a tinned puppy food, which we introduce when the puppies are about three weeks of age or a little younger. For the first feed the mince is held in the hand and a small amount is taken between the finger and thumb so that it can be offered to each puppy. Almost instantly the puppy will smell the meat and begin to suck it from your finger, but don't be tempted to give too much even if he wants more. Give each puppy a little and then let them continue to feed from their mother. Repeat this two or three times in the first day, then increase to five times for the second day. By the third day the puppies will readily take the mince from a feeding bowl.

We then moisten the meat with warm water, gravy or milk, and continue this procedure for a further week. Do not, however, be tempted to give the puppies excessive quantities of cow's milk as the

Ch. Wyburn Rhula of Oldwell.

lactose content in this milk can cause severe diarrhoea. Vary the meats used between beef, lamb, and chicken, and feed it raw if you wish (make sure that it has been passed as fit for human consumption before you do so). As an alternative, you could feed macaroni cheese or rice pudding made with goat's milk. At all times allow the puppies free access to fresh, clean drinking water.

By the end of the second week we add to the diet fish, eggs, and a small amount of top-quality wholemeal puppy meal. Pilchards, mackerel, or herrings, mashed and mixed in with the puppy meal, make an excellent alternative that is rich in both vitamins A and D. Finally, add crushed multivitamin tablets to one meal daily together with brewer's yeast and garlic powder. Once per week, especially in the winter, give each puppy 3ml of cod-liver oil.

Kennel Club Registration

The puppies will need to be registered with The Kennel Club. For this you will need the Application for Litter Registration by the Breeder (Form 1), which should be obtained direct from The Kennel Club before you take your bitch for mating. The section of the form appertaining to the stud-dog must be completed and signed by the owner of the stud dog at the time of mating.

As the breeder of the litter it is your responsibility to complete the rest of the form and to send it, together with a cheque covering the appropriate fee, to The Kennel Club. It is advisable to send it when the litter is about three weeks of age so that the registration certificates should be back with you before the puppies are ready to go to their new homes.

10

Ailments and Diseases

Unfortunately, at some time in your dog's life there is the possibility that he may suffer illness or injury. The intention of this chapter is to bring to your attention some of the problems you may be confronted with so that you are able to identify symptoms at an early stage.

As a devoted dog owner you will no doubt know your own dog and should be able to distinguish the tell-tale signs when he is not his usual bouncy self. As owners it is our responsibility to seek veterinary attention before the condition deteriorates and puts the dog through pain or discomfort. Remember that most conditions have a far greater chance of being treated successfully if they are caught in time.

All responsible dog owners should keep a basic first-aid kit for use in emergencies. This should include bandages, cotton wool, curved scissors, a thermometer, sticking-plasters, preparations to treat stings and bites, and a mild antiseptic.

Abscesses

Bacterial infection or the presence of an irritant within the tissue usually causes abscesses. Whenever the cause is bacterial, white blood cells will engulf the bacteria in an attempt to kill them off. Pus will then form from the dead bacteria and dead white blood cells, together with dead tissue cells and fluid from the blood vessels. Thus the abscess will continue to grow until it either bursts or has to be lanced.

Treatment involves either administering antibiotics or opening up the abscess, and should be carried out by a vet. Do not open an abscess yourself as there is a high risk of re-infection; in any case, a general anaesthetic will probably be needed. If for any reason you do have to perform this procedure then strict attention to cleanliness is the golden rule, particularly if the abscess is close to an orifice.

Anaemia

Primary anaemia is the failure of the body to produce haemoglobin in sufficient quantities. This may be due either to a lack of iron, cobalt, copper, or vitamins in the diet, or to chronic sepsis. Secondary anaemia is the result of severe haemorrhaging and its causes are many and varied, including to a lesser degree the loss of blood from constant attack by external parasites.

Symptoms are a staggering gait, pallid mucous membranes, a rapid, weak pulse, cold extremities, and shivering. If the cause is injury the dog will deteriorate rapidly, but when it is the result of an underlying disease the symptoms may develop much more gradually. The dog becomes dull and listless, exhaustion follows even after only very little exercise, and the mucous membranes become paler. There is a loss of appetite, the coat loses condition, and in severe cases there are heart palpitations.

Treatment usually involves adding vitamin B12 to the diet, or copper, cobalt, or iron if a deficiency in these trace elements is the cause. Another good remedy can be extracts of liver.

Anal Gland Complaints

Signs of anal gland problems are constant licking of the rectum, chewing and nibbling either side of the tail, or dragging the posterior along the ground. If your dog chews itself near its tail then first eliminate the possibility of flea infestation. If not attended to promptly anal gland problems can result in very painful abscesses which will require veterinary attention.

Treatment for anal gland conditions is usually carried out by your vet, although it is not beyond the capabilities of the average dog owner. If you do attempt to clear the glands of their contents yourself, have someone hold the dog still whilst you do so. Arm yourself with a large wad of cotton wool, and begin by placing this wad over the dog's anus. The next step is to place your index finger and thumb over the cotton wool and to either side of the anus slightly below the centre. Squeeze with firm pressure to accomplish the job, possibly repeating the process two or three times to release the compaction. Always stand to one side of the dog as there may be a chance that you have not positioned the cotton wool correctly so that you are engulfed in the foul-smelling wax-type fluid as it is released.

If you experience any difficulties or if the dog shows excessive pain, then discontinue and seek veterinary attention. If this process has to be repeated regularly, then it is possible that your vet may suggest that the glands are removed surgically.

There are several suggestions as to why any dog has to suffer this indignity. In the majority of cases the culprit is probably diet, although it can also be attributed to infection or the presence of foreign bodies such as grass seeds, which can cause a blockage in the ducts of the glands. With regards to the diet, feeding excess quantities of soft foods will not provide satisfactory amounts of fibre, and so may cause the problem. If your dog is continually passing soft motions, then the anal glands are not functioning correctly.

Appetite, Lack of

There can be many causes for this, one of which is that the genetic make-up of the dog is such that he only needs to eat like a sparrow. As long as his intake satisfies his own individual body metabolism, then there is no cause for alarm. Further reasons for lack of appetite are that it could be a symptom of illness, such as intestinal problems, digestive disorders, a bad tooth, an object lodged between the teeth, or a sore throat. Deficiency of the B-complex vitamins can also be responsible for a diminished appetite.

It is not uncommon for a dog to not eat every day. If, however, this persists for more than two days and you cannot find any logical explanation for it, and if the dog cannot be tempted to eat his favourite tasty morsel, then seek veterinary advice.

Arthritis

The most common form of arthritis is osteoarthritis, which is a degenerative and progressive deterioration of the joints rather than an inflammatory disease, and is the result of a combination of ageing and mechanical processes. It would appear that the joints most commonly affected in the dog are the hips, and stifle- and elbow joints. Although naturally it is more common in older dogs, arthritis can occur in younger dogs, usually as the result of injury.

Dogs suffering from arthritis should be kept away from cold and damp conditions, and elderly dogs can be provided with a coat during the winter months. Dogs suffering from osteoarthritis should never be overexercised as this can cause undue pain (as the condition deteriorates the dog will find movement increasingly painful). Under no circumstances should you allow your dog to become overweight as this will place extra stress and strain on the joints.

The majority of available treatments seem to involve the administration of analgesics. In extreme conditions surgery is a consideration, but in all cases you must be guided by your vet.

Canine Parvovirus

This is a viral infection of the intestines, very similar to a severe form of gastro-enteritis. The symptoms are a refusal to eat or drink, vomiting, diarrhoea, and listlessness, and the dog will appear completely depressed. Usually the first sign observed by the owner is that the dog loses his appetite, becomes very quiet, and looks slightly dejected. Soon after this diarrhoea may develop (this is the one symptom that is always present) and vomiting can occur at about the same time or shortly afterwards. As the disease progresses, the frequency of the diarrhoea will increase. In severe cases the diarrhoea will be very loose and perhaps bloodstained, and quite often will have a vile smell about it, reminiscent of old rusty tins. There is still a high mortality rate with this disease, and dogs often become so ill that the only humane thing left to do is to have them put down. In virtually all cases such suffering can be avoided if the dogs are vaccinated against the disease.

An infected dog requires immediate veterinary assistance, and in some cases may be administered a drug to help prevent vomiting. Treatment is mainly of a supportive nature, and involves giving fluids to combat the dehydration caused by the constant vomiting and diarrhoea, along with extra vitamins. An effective way of replacing the fluids is via an intravenous drip. The degree to which a dog is dehydrated can easily be assessed by gently pinching and raising, between finger and thumb, the skin over the top of the shoulders and then releasing it. In a fully hydrated dog this skin should return to normal almost instantly, in the dehydrated dog it will return more slowly, and in a severely dehydrated dog it will not return at all. Any dogs suffering from canine parvovirus should be isolated.

Canine Viral Hepatitis

There are two types of canine viral hepatitis: CAV 1, which affects the liver, eyes, kidney, and respiratory system; and CAV 2, which is associated only with respiratory disease. It is possible for a dog to be infected and yet not display any symptoms – in such dogs the condition can only be confirmed by laboratory tests. Some of the more common symptoms are a high temperature, anaemia, lethargy, a weak, irregular pulse, vomiting accompanied by a tenderness of the abdomen, and diarrhoea. It can also happen that a dog displays no symptoms whatsoever and yet within twenty-four hours it is dead. As with canine parvovirus, adequate vaccines are available to prevent this disease, and so it should not occur. Any dog in whom it does occur should be isolated.

Cleft Palates

This is usually a hereditary defect and takes the form of a hole in the palate. A further possible cause is a dietary deficiency in the bitch during pregnancy.

It is not uncommon for puppies with a cleft palate also to have a hare-lip; this is the incomplete formation of the upper lip, in which there is a gap between the two halves of the lip. Puppies with either condition cannot suckle and so will die shortly after birth if left to their own devices, but with careful nursing and tube-feeding they can survive until they are old enough to be operated on. As both cleft palates and hare-lips are hereditary defects, any dog displaying them should never be used for breeding.

Cruciate Ligament Complaints

The two cruciate ligaments of the stifle-joint prevent overextension of the joint. Their configuration through and around the stifle joint is that of an 'X', hence their name. Degenerative changes of one or both of these ligaments can give rise to lameness.

The initial stages of the condition can be indicated by intermittent lameness, which generally increases in frequency as the pain increases and the dog takes the weight off the affected leg when standing. In severe cases degeneration can lead to rupture, with the resultant instability of the joint. In the case where both ligaments rupture, the dog will lose all control of the lower portion of the leg, from the joint downwards.

Although this condition is common in most breeds, the most susceptible dogs seem to be those that are engaged in strenuous exercise, those that get little exercise and are then allowed to run riot, and those that carry excessive weight. In all of these situations excess stress can be placed on the ligaments.

The only solution when both ligaments rupture is surgery to repair the rupture. There are various techniques to achieve this, some of which will stretch the existing ligaments and effect a repair in this way, while others will insert an artificial portion of the ligament. In other cases a portion of the leg muscle may be used to repair the damage.

Physiotherapy after surgery is highly beneficial, and subsequently allowing the dog access to controlled swimming can help immensely. However, in some cases strict rest and confinement for a period in excess of eight weeks have proved successful.

Cystitis

This is an inflammation of the urinary bladder, and is far more common in bitches than dogs. Bacterial infection is the most usual cause, although others include the retention of urine over lengthy periods of time. The usual signs are that the dog makes frequent attempts to pass urine but will usually only manage to pass small amounts, which may be bloodstained and may smell offensive.

Treatment usually takes the form of antibiotics once the vet has determined the source of the bacterial infection. It will assist the vet in doing so if you supply a sample of the dog's urine.

Cysts, Interdigital

These are abscesses that appear in the spaces between the dog's toes. There are four main possible causes: there is an infection in the hair follicles; foreign bodies have worked their way under the skin between the toes; the dog is generally run down in condition; or, finally, there is a hereditary factor that predisposes the dog to the condition.

Symptoms are that the dog constantly licks his foot and later shows lameness on that leg. The painful swelling usually found in the upper part of the interdigital space will come to a head and eventually burst, at which time the dog will feel relief. Although it will seem as if the problem has disappeared, unfortunately it often reappears at a later date.

Treatment consists of bathing the affected paw in hot salt water, and in severe cases cauterizing the lining of the cyst. Strict cleanliness should be adhered to afterwards to minimize the chances of reinfection. To prevent the dog constantly licking his foot fit a plastic buster collar. Whichever way the condition is treated, there does seem to be a high incidence of recurrence.

Diabetes Mellitus

Diabetes mellitus is the inability of the body to absorb sugars from the blood. The condition is more likely to develop in older animals, particularly bitches. Symptoms can be vague. One of the first things you may notice is that the dog develops an excessive thirst and consequently passes larger amounts of urine than normal. The dog will look depressed and lose condition and weight, and in some cases there may be vomiting or the development of a cataract on one or both eyes. Diagnosis is usually confirmed by testing the urine or blood for excess sugar.

Although it is a shock to the owner when an old friend develops diabetes, this condition can usually be treated successfully with the aid of insulin injections and a controlled diet. Caring for a diabetic dog can, however, be a time-consuming process. The weight of the dog must be kept as near to the ideal as possible, and to achieve this the diet must be kept under strict control. Fluid intake must also be monitored as an increased thirst could indicate that the condition is becoming unstable.

Distemper

Canine distemper is a viral disease that affects the Canidae and Mustelidae families of animals (those that do not possess retractable claws), and is spread by contact with infected animals. The dog may appear unwell, with a high temperature and decreased appetite. This situation may persist for a number of days, after which time it is not uncommon for the temperature to return to normal for up to two weeks and then rise again. The dog may have a slight cough and display other symptoms of bronchitis, including a discharge of mucous from the nostrils; sometimes this may be accompanied by sneezing. There is also inflammation of the eyes, whereby the mucous membranes become swollen and congested, possibly accompanied by a discharge from the eye. Vomiting and diarrhoea (with blood being passed in extreme cases) can occur when the digestive system is affected. It is also common for numerous secondary infections to occur.

The prognosis for dogs contracting this disease is very poor. Even dogs that make a full recovery commonly suffer damage to the nervous system and are susceptible to fits later in life. As numerous efficient vaccines are available to prevent distemper there is no excuse for it still to be as prevalent as it is. Any dog suspected of suffering from distemper must be isolated.

Ear Complaints

There are several conditions associated with the ears, some of which are more serious than others. With the majority of them the dog will be seen to hang his head to one side and may possibly shake his head. On closer examination you may find an inflamed ear channel and lobe. If the dog is reluctant for you to handle the ear in order to examine it he may be experiencing quite a high degree of pain. In such cases a trip to your vet is usually the most sensible approach, so that he can examine the ear and formulate a diagnosis.

The problem can usually be attributed to an excessive amount of wax, and in these cases the vet will prescribe an ear wash or cleaner, often in liquid form. The cleaner must be poured into the ear canal and massaged so that it reaches into all the folds and crevices. It is then left for a few minutes, during which time it will soften the wax, before being gently but thoroughly cleaned out with the aid of lint or cotton wool until all traces of the wax have been removed. If left unattended, excessive wax can lead to disease and bacterial infections.

The second most common cause of ear problems is the ear mite *Otodectis cyanotis*. The initial symptoms are that the dog shakes his head and scratches his ears, and in severe cases has a discharge from the ears. This discharge is usually the result of a secondary bacterial infection, caused when the earlier symptoms were neglected. There may be occasions when the dog is in so much pain that a general anaesthetic is required before the vet can clean the badly inflamed ear.

Ear problems may also be caused by the presence of foreign bodies. Grass seeds, sand, grit, or any other small objects can become lodged in the ear and hence cause the dog irritation. Again, signs are shaking of the head, scratching the ear, or rubbing the ear against objects in an attempt to obtain relief.

The majority of problems associated with the ears can be greatly minimized by careful and regular attention to the ears. If conditions do arise then veterinary assistance should be sought as correct diagnosis is essential before any treatment can be prescribed. Remember that constant scratching of the ear can cause damage to the earflap in the form of a haematoma, or if the scratching is vigorous lacerations or even tears to the earflap may result. It is therefore important to seek help at the earliest signs of any symptoms.

Ectropion

Ectropion is the opposite of entropion (*see* below), whereby the eyelids and eyelashes turn outwards. This outward turning exposes the conjunctiva, with the resultant possibilities of infection and inflammation. As with entropion, a minor surgical procedure can alleviate the problem.

Entropion

Entropion is a condition of the eye whereby the lashes of the eyelids turn inwards onto the cornea. It would appear that the condition more often affects the lower lid than the upper lid, and is even more rare on both lids. If left untreated it will cause extreme pain and discomfort to the dog, and will eventually cause ulceration of the cornea and possibly blindness.

There have been numerous suggestions as to the causes of entropion, but in our opinion the only two that have any creditability are that it is the result of a hereditary defect, or that it is due to the shape and size of the eye and general configuration of the head. With

186

regards to the causes being hereditary, the situation is still not clear. It has been suggested by Burns and Fraser that the mode of inheritance may be by a simple dominant gene, or possibly a dominant gene with variable expressivity. Other research suggests that the mode of inheritance is of a recessive nature. The second possible cause is that the shape of the eye together with excessive wrinkles of flesh on the head will tend to turn the eyelids into the eye.

The more we have studied this condition, however, the more examples we have found that contradict each of these suggested causes. We have seen dogs that show no hint of entropion, and that have no evidence of the condition in their ancestors for three generations, subsequently produce one or more affected dogs in their litters. We have also known of dogs affected with entropion that have always produced clear offspring when mated. The offspring from one such mating was mated back to the parent; again, none of the offspring from this second generation displayed signs of entropion. As far as the suggestion that overwrinkled heads is a possible cause goes, we have seen extremely heavily wrinkled dogs that were completely free of all signs of entropion. Conversely, we have also seen plain-headed dogs that were affected in both eyes.

In the majority of cases entropion can be detected in dogs as young as four weeks. Unfortunately, however, it is not unknown for the first signs to appear in a dog as old as two years and in some breeds as old as seven years. Surgery is the only permanent solution, and has an almost 100 per cent success rate.

A condition sometimes confused with entropion is dry-eye syndrome. Discharge is also produced from the eyes, but the mucus results from a lack of lubrication over the cornea as insufficient tears are produced. The treatment for dry-eye syndrome consists of the application of substitute tears for the rest of the dog's life.

Hip Dysplasia

The hip joint is a ball and socket construction, firmly held together by a mass of powerful muscles and ligaments. The term hip dysplasia is currently used to describe a number of abnormalities of the acetabulum (socket) and the head of the femur (ball). While several symptoms may indicate the possibility of abnormalities within the joint, such symptoms should only be regarded as a diagnostic aid and not positive proof of a dysplastic joint. It is perfectly possible that some of the symptoms may be indicative of other conditions, and so the only positive confirmation of the condition is by X-ray.

There are various methods employed to calculate the degree of severity of hip dysplasia, but that currently used by the British Veterinary Association in association with The Kennel Club is to sub-divide the hip joint into nine separate features and to assess each of these in turn, awarding a score between 0 (the ideal for each feature) and 6 (the worst). This system allows the breeder more freedom to use their discretion within their breeding programme as he or she can take on board all points.

Although the causes of hip dysplasia are still under debate, they are generally attributed to heredity, nutrition, and environment. The degree apportioned to each of these appears to be approximately of equal proportions. Some breeders have suggested that the main contributory factor to hip dysplasia is diet, and that dogs reared on less than the optimum food intake will not develop the condition. We believe that this is not only incorrect but detrimental to the well-being of the young dog. While it is good practice to keep a young dog in a fit condition, without any excess weight, this can be achieved by feeding a correctly balanced diet in the desired quantities. By reducing the food intake you are likely to cause far more problems.

Another strongly held view is that a restriction of exercise during adolescence or confinement of the dog until adolescence has passed will again reduce the likelihood of hip dysplasia. It is true that at birth all puppies are free of hip dysplasia, and so if the dog never uses the hips through playing and exercising then wear and tear on the hip joint will be minimal. However, as the hip joint is held together primarily by the muscle mass surrounding it, if a dog is con-fined and deprived of normal exercise then there will be muscle wastage and consequently more subluxation. In any case, there is lit-tle logic in depriving a dog of a natural way of life, including normal activities such as running, jumping, and playing, in the hope of slightly improving the hip joint.

It is also becoming common for some breeders to concentrate on producing dogs with good hips at the expense of the rest of the dog. It is surely better to produce dogs that are typical of the breed and that have trouble-free hips than to produce a dog with a perfect set of hips that looks nothing like a Bullmastiff. After all, if you want a dog with perfect hips at the expense of everything else then you have only to breed racing Greyhounds.

Anyone wishing to know more about canine hip dysplasia should read *Genetics of the Dog* by Malcolm B. Willis and *Canine Hip Dysplasia* by Fred L. Lanting (*see* Bibliography), both of which make the subject understandable to the layman.

Kennel Cough

The majority of cases of kennel cough are contracted at boarding kennels (hence the name), dog shows, ringcraft training clubs, or parks – in fact, anywhere in which dogs congregate in close proximity to one another. The disease is highly infectious, so any affected dog must be isolated from others. And since it is caused by any of several viruses and bacteria, vaccination for *Bordetella bronchiseptica* (the principal cause) cannot guarantee total protection.

The first sign is a little rasping cough or huff, usually noticeable when the dog becomes excited, but easily missed when the dog is lying quietly or asleep. If there is a secondary infection a green-coloured mucus may seep from the nostrils. We have almost lost two dogs to such a secondary infection resulting from the *Bordetella bronchiseptica* bacterium getting into their lungs. Their recovery was only achieved by a two-hourly treatment of steam and inhalants to relieve the congestion from their lungs, together with the administration of antibiotics to combat the bacteria.

There is no instant cure for kennel cough. The use of antibiotics alone helps very little, as in the majority of cases the cause is an airborne virus. Treatment for the most part consists of decongestants, cough medicine to relieve the symptoms of coughing, and occasionally antibiotics to deal with any secondary infection. We have found that one of the best ways of dealing with kennel cough is to put the animal in a warm, steamy environment such as the kitchen or bathroom. Place a warmed receptacle containing a decongestant mixed with water in the room; the resultant inhalation should clear the nasal passage and bronchial tubes. In an adult dog treat the actual cough with 10ml of cough syrup given three times a day.

The incubation period for kennel cough varies from three to ten days, and the coughing can last for more than three weeks. However, it is still infectious at this stage so you should allow a lapse of at least six weeks after the commencement of the cough before letting your dog mix with others.

Leptospirosis

The two types of leptospirosis bacteria most commonly associated with the dog are *Leptospira canicola* and *L. icterohaemorrhagiae*. Leptospirosis is a very serious infection and can also be fatal to man. It can be prevented by vaccination.

L. canicola can present various symptoms, including loss of appetite, depression, fever (either with or without excessive thirst and vomiting), loss of weight, and an ulcerated tongue accompanied by a foul odour. The disease progresses from the blood in the early stages to the kidneys at a later stage. Death can occur from kidney failure or chronic interstitial nephritis.

L. icterohaemorrhagiae is the other form of the disease most commonly associated with dogs. Transmission of this disease is effected either by contamination from the urine of an animal that is carrying the disease, or, in rare cases in terrier-type dogs, from killing rats that are infected. The disease can also be contracted through abrasions on the skin. The symptoms displayed are a high fever, depression, reluctance to eat, and a severe loss of weight. Kidney and liver damage follow, and in a high percentage of cases jaundice is therefore seen. Death can occur as a result of excessive damage to the liver and kidneys.

Pyometra

This is a collection of pus in the uterus, and is caused either by the introduction of infection during a natural service or after giving birth, or from a previous metritis that has not completely cleared. It has also been known for the administration of oestrogen, used in the case of a misalliance, to lay the foundations for this problem. The condition is most commonly seen in the bitch approximately six weeks after the commencement of her season, and although it is more common in older bitches it can occur at any age. There are two forms of pyometra: the open form, in which the pus has a means of escape; and the closed form, in which the pus is trapped within the womb.

One of the first and most obvious symptoms is excessive thirst, followed by frequent attempts at urinating. Further symptoms are depression, a rise in temperature, signs of pain and discomfort, loss of appetite, and, with the open form of pyometra, an offensive discharge from the vulva. If all or any of these symptoms is present you should seek veterinary advice immediately.

Of the two manifestations of pyometra, the open form is most easily noticed and treated. Treatment consists of the administration of antibiotics plus a drug that causes the womb to contract, combined with the use of a two-way catheter to wash out the pus. Failing this, an ovariohysterectomy will be performed. It is imperative that treatment is delayed no longer than is absolutely necessary as otherwise toxaemia may develop.

Vaginal Hyperplasia (Prolapse)

The breeder is usually first aware of this problem when he notices a swollen mass protruding from the bitch's vulva, usually a few days after she has come into season. It is believed that the cause for such a prolapse is hormonal stimulation.

With regards to treatment, in the majority of cases this is unnecessary – other than to keep the mass clean and to avoid damage – as the mass will usually shrink back to normal by itself as the bitch progresses through her season and passes ovulation. Most vets will suggest that the bitch should be spayed to prevent a recurrence. If the owner intends to breed from this bitch, then providing the mass subsides sufficiently by the time the bitch is ready to mate, an experienced stud-dog is chosen, and plenty of lubrication is used, it should be possible to effect a normal mating.

11

The Bullmastiff Around the World

Australia

(By Andrew Burt)

The history of the Bullmastiff in Australia spans nearly fifty years, and can attribute its firm foundations to the early introduction of some very good specimens. Naturally, as a newly introduced breed the Bullmastiff took a long time to gain popularity, and as a result breeding remained limited until the 1970s. However, the dedicated effort of breeders, combined with the influence of several significant imports over the last twenty years, has led the breed to flourish. Today, there are some excellent specimens, and judges are far more familiar with the desired type and characteristics of the breed. We see sound breed-judging exhibitions and greater instances of good specimens being rewarded for their attributes in group competition.

Early Imports

The very first recorded importation of a Bullmastiff to Australia occurred in 1949 when Mr C. J. Ewing migrated to Victoria from England and brought with him a Bullmastiff named Major. This first arrival was soon followed by several more imports from England. Mr J. F. Nixon of New South Wales imported the brindle dog Brynmount Samson (by Perigrine of Harbex out of Brunwins Sally) in 1950. This dog was followed by the bitch Wish of Harbex, and the two formed the foundation of the Bulmar Kennel. Mr Ewing also imported Blunderbus of Bulmas (by Ch. Master of Marbette out of Ch. Bright Gem of Bulmas).

These first arrivals were followed by a number of very significant imports during the 1950s and 1960s, leading to the establishment of

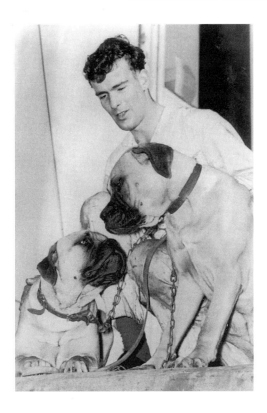

Mr Andrew Burt with two Bulstaff imports to Australia, Austral. Ch. Bulstaff Jellicoe (left), and Austral. Ch. Bulstaff Maid Marion.

kennels that were very influential in the development of the breed in Australia. Mr J. Russell imported Austral. Ch. Boomerang of Bulmas, Austral. Ch. Bush Lass of Bulmas, Bullimby of Bulmas, and Bonza of Bulmas, and used these animals to form the basis of his Mastodon Kennel. Mr G. Fortune of the Behemoth Kennel imported Bulstaff Delilah of Buttonoak (by Ch. Antony of Buttonoak out of Bulstaff Felicity), while Mrs G. Flitcroft imported Roger of Wighay and Wild Honey of Woodhaven as the beginning of her Jacksdale Kennel, and Dr R. Lakes imported Bulstaff Jodo of Vorsodene. The well-known pair Austral. Ch. Bulstaff Jellicoe and Austral. Ch. Bulstaff Maid Marion were imported by Mrs J. Stevenson and Mr B. Lummis respectively. Mrs Stevenson went on to import Bulstaff Black Prince, who was responsible for the emergence of many of the early brindle Bullmastiffs in the 1970s.

Three UK champion Bullmastiffs have been imported to Australia. The first was Ch. Purston Harvest Gold (by Ch. Frederick of Kelwall out of Naukeen Viola), imported by Mr F. Frencham. Mr Frencham also imported the second dog, Ch. & Austral. Ch. Naukeen Night Ranger (by Maxstoke Tegwyn out of Naukeen Enchantress), who, at the time of writing, was the only such titled Bullmastiff in the country. Most recently, in late 1997, Mr and Mrs P. Abela imported the bitch Ch. Pryderi Simansana (by Ch. Graecia Mercury out of Austral. Ch. Graecia Araminta).

Various kennels were producing Australian-bred dogs during the 1960s.

The Mastodon Kennel of Mr J. Russell produced many dogs with strong bones and typical heads. The influence of Mr C. Leeke's Bulmas breeding was most evident in progeny from this kennel, and these lines are behind most Australian-bred Bullmastiffs today.

The Behemoth Kennel of Mr G. Fortune produced a significant number of puppies combining the Bulmas and Bulstaff lines that had been imported to Australia from the UK.

The Bisonte Kennel of Mr B. Lummis produced quality animals from the mating of Austral. Ch. Bulstaff Maid Marion to Austral. Ch. Behemoth Count. Austral. Ch. Bisonte Gay Cabellero, owned by Mr Lummis, was arguably one of the most notable of these.

The Masterville Kennel of Mrs J. Stevenson produced puppies that combined the early Australian breeding, and also produced litters with her Bulstaff imports.

The Bullbart Kennel of Mr E. Bartosy imported Elgar of Kelwall and Detta of Kelwall. Detta (by Ch. Oldwell Toby of Studbergh out of Cortella of Kelwall) produced puppies by Austral. Ch. Mastodon Minotaurus that were significant in the breeding that took place in the 1970s.

The Harliz Kennel of Mrs N. Laker in Tasmania imported Penny Princess (by Lingmell Thunderstorm out of Goodstock Top Notcher). This bitch was mated to Austral. Ch. Bulstaff Jellicoe, and produced one of the top-winning dogs of the time, Austral. Ch. Harliz Royal Sovereign. Harliz puppies were also significant in the development of the breed in New Zealand.

The Barndale Kennel of Mr and Mrs G. Shaw used Behemoth lines to produce some of the early champions.

By the 1970s, Bullmastiff numbers had swelled significantly and there were quite a few interested and dedicated breeders. However, three kennels seem to characterize the breed development during this time.

The first is the Bullmaster Kennel of Mr and Mrs P. Wright in Victoria, which was founded with the bitch Nairobie Tranquility (by

Austral. Ch. Bisonte Gay Caballero out of Austral. Ch. Mastodon Malabete). To my knowledge Bullmaster is the longest-established and longest-working kennel in the country, and many of the quality puppies it produced in the early days helped with the formation of other kennels in both Australia and New Zealand. Some of the Wrights' more notable products include Austral. Ch. Bullmaster Desiree (owned by Mr and Mrs T. Merritt), NZ Ch. Bullmaster Mason (Imp. Aust.; owned by Mr J. Banks), Austral. Ch. Bullmaster Big Guns (owned by Mrs P. Quinn), and Austral. Ch. Bullmaster Sweet Melody (retained by the Wrights).

The Wideacre Kennel of Mr and Mrs T. Merritt in Victoria was probably the most prolific kennel in Australia during the 1970s. Breeding began with the purchase of litter-sisters Bullbart Amanda and Bullbart Annette (by Austral. Ch. Mastodon Minotaurus out of Austral. Ch. Detta of Kelwall (Imp. UK)). These bitches were mated to Bulstaff Black Prince (Imp. UK) and produced large litters early in the 1970s. Many of the winning Bullmastiffs of the era carried the Wideacre prefix and became the basis for other smaller kennels emerging at the time. Some of the notable products of Wideacres

Austral. Ch. Bullmaster Sweet Melody.

195

include Austral. Ch. Wideacres Urfi CDX (owned by Mr H. Planke), NZ Ch. Wideacres Witches Brew' (Imp. Aust.; owned by Mr and Mrs B. Powley), and Wideacres Ismael (owned by Ms C. Gilmour and Mr G. Warnock), the first Bullmastiff to win an All-Breeds Best in Show in Australia.

The Nightwatch Kennel of Ms C. Gilmour in Western Australia, based upon Bullmaster and Wideacre stock, used Bullmaster Pandora as its foundation bitch. Although this kennel was disadvantaged by its location (a remote area on the northwestern Australian coast), it invested a great deal in terms of travel and money to develop a line. Nightwatch has produced many winning Bullmastiffs, and later breeding revolved around three UK bitch imports: Double Florin of Colom, Juno of Colom, and Austral. Ch. Pughill Little Nell. Nightwatch has produced two All-Breeds Best in Show winners, together with a number of quality bitches that have gone on to produce well for other Australian kennels, including Bullmaster and Cambalup.

The 1980s were also a time of expansion and importation. Once again, a small number of kennels dominated the decade.

The Bulwaren Kennel of Mrs R. Van Blommestein in Victoria began breeding in the early 1980s, and very successfully combined the lines of Harliz, Bulstaff, and Copperfield with the very first Bulwaren litters. When Austral. Ch. Bulwaren Jackson (a result of this combination) was mated to Austral. Ch. Rose Queen of Colom (Imp. UK), the bloodlines really clicked and many top specimens resulted. The kennel's line was further enhanced with the importation of Austral. Ch. Colom Donald (Imp. UK). Bulwaren has since gone on to produce some twenty champions, with a particularly strong lineage of champion-quality bitches that have won at speciality shows throughout Australia.

The Treebrook Kennel of Mr and Mrs B. Marion of South Australia flourished during the decade. The original stock was based upon two brood-bitches carrying Colom, Oldwell, and Bulwaren lines. These lines were merged very successfully and have produced a line of fine show specimens. Treebrook breeding has now culminated in the winning brother and sister team of Austral. Ch. Treebrook Coral Gum and Austral. Ch. Treebrook Raywood, both of whom have held their own in competitions throughout Australia.

The Bullpower Kennel of Mr and Mrs D. Butler of New South Wales produced a large number of dogs during the 1980s. Along with the Volontaire Kennel of Mr J. Veenstra in New South Wales,

Austral. Ch. Vanetta Cindy.

the kennel was based upon brood-bitches from the very successful Vanetta litter bred in Canberra and sired by Lombardy Taurus (Imp. UK). Bullpower merged these lines with Austral. Ch. Maxstoke Norton (Imp. UK; by Ch. Graecia Centaur out of Maxstoke Cleopatra) to develop a very recognizable type of Bullmastiff. The dogs were mainly reds, and they included numerous champions such as Austral. Ch. Bullpower Olympia, Austral. Ch. Bullpower Montgomery, and Austral. Ch. Bullpower Jaguar. Volontaire also produced some very notable Bullmastiffs, of whom Austral. Ch.

Volontair Formidable, Austral. Ch. Volontair Zara, Austral. Ch. Volontair Missouri, and Austral. Ch. Volontair Simasana come to mind.

Since the start of the 1990s the breed has really gained in strength and popularity, and there are many kennels worthy of mention. New South Wales is certainly well ahead in terms of numbers, and both the Powerbulmas Kennel of Mr and Mrs P. Abela and the Masbull Kennel of Mr and Mrs T. Allen are very dominant in terms of their size. Just a few of the many kennels that have emerged during this time include Kangala of Mr and Mrs K. Cannon in New South Wales, Bulvadere of Mr and Mrs I. Chandler in South Australia, Lilacglen of Mr and Mrs J. Hartmann in New South Wales, Bulconan of Mr and Mrs L. Cleghorn in Victoria, Nightmaster of Mr and Mrs P. Alexander in South Australia, Soloshel of Ms P. Williams in New South Wales, and Cambalup of Mr and Mrs D. Grimshaw in New South Wales.

With the advent of frozen semen, many great dogs from across the world can now be used as sires in Australia without having to make

Austral. Ch. Bulstaff Tiger Tim (UK imp.) with Mrs J. Stevenson.

the trip themselves. There has been limited success so far with semen imported from lines that include Blackslate, Oldwell, and Graecia in the UK. However, I am sure that this process will continue to improve so that conscientious Australian breeders are given access to successful lines from around the world in order that they may enhance their own lines.

Influential Imports

The historical influence of the early imports to Australia has been very strong and provided the breed with a sound grounding (*see* above). Since that time a great number of dogs have been imported to the country, with varying degrees of influence on the breed due to many factors. In my opinion, there have been several very noteworthy imports (all from the UK) over the last two decades that deserve special mention. These include the following.

Austral. Ch. Bulstaff Tiger Tim (by Wyaston Tudor Herald out of Crowhurst Kummel of Bulstaff), imported by Mrs J. Stevenson of Victoria in 1974, provided a much-needed boost to the brindle bloodlines in the country and produced some excellent offspring. These

Ch. Colom Jumbo.

included the well-regarded Austral. Ch. Abbeygrove Lord Louis and Bulwaren Kennel's foundation bitch, Austral. Ch. Harliz Brindle Princess.

Austral. Ch. Maxstoke Norton (by Ch. Graecia Centaur out of Maxstoke Cleopatra), imported by Mr S. Nicholas of New South Wales in 1985, won well in the New South Wales show ring, including CCs at the Sydney Royal. He was also the sire of many champion offspring.

Austral. Ch. Rose Queen of Colom (by Ch. Colom Jumbo out of Caiterlea Annette), imported by Mrs R. Van Blommestein of Victoria

Austral. Ch. Oldwell Laird.

in 1983, proved to be a successful show bitch, winning Speciality CCs and many Royal CCs. However, her real influence in Australia was as a brood-bitch – she produced some eleven champions and the foundation stock for several other notable Australian kennels. It is a fitting testament to her influence that her progeny and grandchildren have won Best Exhibit in Show and/or Runner-Up to Best Exhibit in Show at the Victorian Bullmastiff Club Speciality every year since 1987.

Austral. Ch. Pughill Little Nell (by Berick of Codshall out of Maymar Lady Ursula), imported by Mrs M. Cochrane of Western Australia in 1985 and then bought by Ms C. Gilmour soon after, produced many quality offspring. These included two All-Breeds Best in Show winners. Her offspring have also gone on to produce well for other Australian kennels.

Austral. Ch. Oldwell Laird (by Ch. Wyburn Rula of Oldwell out of Ch. Sylva of Oldwell), imported by Mr and Mrs T. Clarke of South Australia in 1985, did an incredible amount of winning in the ring, including a run of four CCs and Best in Breeds at the Adelaide Royal. He produced many champion progeny, all of which carried his very distinctive stamp of type.

Austral. Ch. Colom Donald (by Maxstoke Gwylym out of Brittania of Colom), imported by Mrs R. Van Blommestein of Victoria in 1988, was a very successful show dog. He won several Speciality CCs, including the Best in Show at the Inaugural Championship Show of the Bullmastiff Club of New South Wales under the late Dr H. Spira. He has produced many quality offspring, especially when combined with Austral. Ch. Rose Queen of Colom or her Bulwaren daughters.

Austral. Ch. Morvern Eachan (by Bronson of Bunsoro out of Morvern Dulcie), imported by Mr J. Klok of New South Wales in 1990, has won well under breed specialists, including the Dog CC under Mr A. Rostron of the UK at the 1992 New South Wales Speciality. This dog was well used at stud and produced many winning progeny, including Austral. Ch. Bullvalour Jack the Ripa, who won Best in Show at the New South Wales Speciality and the CC, Best in Breed, and Best in Group at the Sydney Royal in 1997.

Austral. Ch. Graecia Pryderi (by Ch. Graecia Centaur out of Ch. Graecia Celestine), imported by Mr and Mrs G. Frowen in 1991 and obtained soon after by Mr and Mrs T. Allen, has won a Speciality Best in Show. He has produced many champion progeny that are now winning in the ring.

Austral. Ch. Bulwaren Silver Fox.

Outstanding Dogs

Today, the Bullmastiff population in Australia is quite large, and one can expect to see a good number of exhibits in the show ring, particularly at each state's speciality show. To my mind there are several Bullmastiffs that at the time of writing stand out as worthy of mention.

Austral. Ch. Powerbulmas Pezaz Obargo (by Austral. Ch. Bruin Gladiator out of Bygunya Becky Dee) was Best in Show at the Inaugural Speciality Show of the South Australian Championship Show under Mrs E. Evans of the UK. He has also won two All-Breeds Runner-Up in Show awards.

Austral. Ch. Bullmaster Sweet Melody (by Austral. Ch. Nightbeauty Benson Lee out of Austral. Ch. Nightwatch Sweet

Austral. Ch. Treebrook Satinwood, Bullmastiff of the Year (South Australia) 1997.

Embrace) is a quality bitch and the winner of two Speciality Best in Show awards.

Austral. Ch. Bulwaren Silver Fox (by Austral. Ch. Bulwaren Earl O Plenty out of Austral. Ch. Bulwaren Shiralee) is a bitch that has won much within the breed in Victoria, and is greatly admired by the Bullmastiff fraternity. She presents a beautiful picture of Bullmastiff type when standing.

Austral. Ch. Treebrook Raywood (by Austral. Ch. Treebrook Bloodwood out of Austral. Ch. Treebrook Satinwood) has, along with his sister Austral. Ch. Treebrook Coral Gum, won many awards, including a Speciality Best in Show and a Royal Best in Breed. He is much admired as a typical, very sound Bullmastiff.

Austral. Ch. Cambrai Pryde 'n' Paegent (by Austral. Ch. Graecia Pryderi (Imp. UK) out of Austral. Ch. Masbull Lady Bollin) is a very energetic and typical Bullmastiff. He has won a Speciality Best in Show and an All-Breeds Best in Group, when he also went on to win Runner-Up to Best in Show.

In the twenty-six years I have been involved with the breed I have seen a good number of dogs that could be classed as 'great'. My list of all-time greats (below) contains three Bullmastiffs that, in my opinion, exemplify the Bullmastiff Standard and type.

Austral. Ch. Harliz Royal Sovereign (by Austral. Ch. Bulstaff Jellicoe (Imp. UK) out of Penny Princess (Imp. UK)) was born in 1969 and owned by Mrs J. Stevenson. He was a magnificent red dog standing 27in (66cm) tall. He possessed a beautiful head, was very sound, and showed himself off to advantage. In the show ring he remained virtually unbeaten, and he sired numerous quality litters that feature in many of the pedigrees of today's winning dogs.

Austral. Ch. Abbeygrove Lord Louis (by Austral. Ch. Bulstaff Tiger Tim (Imp. UK) out of Bullmaster Sandy), owned and bred by Mrs D. Mulham and born in 1979, was a top-class brindle dog. He moved better than most of his contemporaries and carried a very typical head. Louis won four Best in Shows in a row at the Victorian Speciality (this was the only Australian speciality show conducted at this time).

Austral. Ch. Bulwaren Stephanie (by Ch. Bulwaren Jackson out of Austral. Ch. Rose Queen of Colom (Imp. UK)), born in 1986, was bred and owned by Mrs R. Van Blommestein. Stephanie was a small bitch who possessed outstanding type and movement. Mrs M. Cox from the UK rewarded her virtues by her awarding her Bitch CC and Runner-Up Best in Show at the 1989 Victorian Speciality.

Breed Clubs in Australia

The Bullmastiff Club of Victoria was formed in 1964, and conducted its first open parade in 1972 and first championship show in 1974. In 1998 the club held its twenty-fifth championship show. For many years Victoria remained central to the development of the Bullmastiff in Australia, but during the 1980s other states began to gather strength and form breed societies, so that there are now four affiliated Bullmastiff clubs in Australia. The Bullmastiff Club of New South Wales was affiliated in 1988, and held its first championship show in 1991. The Bullmastiff Club of South Australia was also formed in 1988, and held its first championship show in 1997. Western Australia formed a club in 1993 and held its first championship show in 1998.

The year 1997 saw the formation and affiliation of the National Bullmastiff Council of Australia. The first Bullmastiff National Show will be conducted by the Bullmastiff Club of Victoria (subject to Australian National Kennel Council approval) in 1999, marking the turn of the century and heralding a new era of unity and communication for Bullmastiffs and Bullmastiff fanciers across Australia.

New Zealand

(By Keith Warren)

The Bullmastiff in New Zealand is a relatively new breed, although in the New Zealand Kennel Club archives is recorded a Bullmastiff named Caeser, a dog born on 1 August 1948 and bred by Mrs S. Lowes. Very little is known about this dog.

The first imports (from Australia) were Behemoth Crusader, a fawn dog born on 1 May 1960, and NZ Ch. Behemoth Regal Duchess, a fawn bitch born on 25 September 1961 and bred by Mr and Mrs Fortune. The two dogs were mated together without success. However, Regal Duchess, owned by Mrs K. Matenga, became the first New Zealand Champion Bullmastiff on 3 April 1965 and was also obedience trained to Test B.

Other early Australian imports included Wideacres Nero, a fawn dog born on 6 April 1971 who sired no registered litters, and his litter-brother Wideacres Rebel Rouser, a brindle dog (by Bulstaff Black Prince (Imp. UK) out of Bullbart Amanda). Both dogs were bred by Mr and Mrs T. Merritt. Rebel Rouser sired one litter, born on 29 September 1976, out of Bullmaster Jennel (Imp. Aust.), a fawn bitch born on 12 July 1972. Bullmaster Jennel was bred by Mr and Mrs P. Wright (by Austral. Ch. Bullbart Achilles out of Nairobe Tranquility) for Mr and Mrs Barnett of Sunnymead Kennels.

In 1972 the first UK imports arrived. These included Knightguard MacGregor, a red dog born on 2 October 1971 (by Ch. Showell Yibor out of Showell Talina), bred by Mrs J. McKnight; and Minnoch of Minnyhive, a red bitch born on 1 November 1971 (by Ch. Showell Yibor out of Showell Xenda), bred by Major A. Flattery. Both dogs were owned by Mr W. Hubber, and together they produced two litters with the Knightguard prefix, born on 26 June 1973 and 17 August 1974.

The first New Zealand-bred registered litter was by Wideacres Pharoah (Imp. Aust.), a fawn dog born on 5 November 1971 (by Bulstaff Black Prince (Imp. UK) out of Bullbart Amanda), out of Harliz Silver Princess (Imp. Aust), a fawn bitch born on 6 April 1972 (by Harliz Royal Sovereign out of Penny Princess (Imp. UK). The litter was bred by Mr W. Bradley, and included NZ Ch. Blairgowie Marquis, a fawn bitch born on 22 May 1973, who became the country's first home-bred champion on 11 September 1974.

NZ Ch. Wideacres Witches Brew (Imp. Aust.), a fawn bitch born on 8 May 1972 (by Wideacres Shariff out of Bullmaster Desiree), was the foundation bitch for the Arapeti Kennels of Mr and Mrs B. Powley. She was mated to Knightguard MacGregor and produced the red dog NZ Ch. Bobby of Arapeti on 21 March 1974. Bobby became the Powleys' first home-bred champion on 7 June 1975.

NZ Ch. Vance of Bullmanor, Best in Show (Dominion Bullmastiff Club) 1997.

NZ Ch. Oakcroft First Edition, Best in Show (Dominion Bullmastiff Club) in 1993, 1995 and 1996.

NZ Ch. Blairgowie Marquis became the foundation bitch for Dr and Mrs A. Whyte of Mangaroa Kennels. She was mated to NZ Ch. Bobby of Arapeti and on 22 January 1975 produced NZ Ch. Duke Ominuim of Mangaroa, who became the Whyte's first home-bred champion on 23 January 1977. Mangaroa Kennels imported NZ Ch. Copperfield Ham Peggotty, a fawn dog born on 2 January 1975 (by Maverick of Oldwell of Copperfield out of Copperfield Flora Finching) bred by Mr and Mrs G. Warren. Ham Peggotty sired a litter with Marquis, and also sired two litters born on 12 May 1978 and 20 November 1978 with the Whyte's second import, Copperfield Susan Clarke (Imp. UK), a red bitch born on 25 May 1976 (by Copperfield Samuel Weller out of Copperfield Ada Clare). Mangaroa and Arapeti are the only kennels from this time still active today.

Bertram of Kelwall (Imp. UK), a brindle dog born on 3 February 1976 (by Ch. Frederick of Kelwall out of Ailsa of Kelwall) bred by Mr and Mrs W. Pratt, was used at stud extensively in New Zealand, siring nine registered litters for Borsdane, Arapeti, Opapa, and Mt Bruce kennels between 1977 and 1985. As such his name is still prominent in New Zealand pedigrees today.

NZ Ch. Bullmaster Ryan (Imp. Aust.), a brindle dog born on 6 April 1976 (by Wideacres Shariff out of Nairobie Tranquility), was the last of the imports in the 1970s and sired three litters for the Yellowoak Kennels.

As the breed became better known and more people became interested in it during the 1980s, more Bullmastiff kennels were established. The gene pool expanded with the importation of dogs from Australia (Nonsinelabor, Volontaire, Kontanka, Bulwaren, Capabull, and Burgowood kennels), the UK (Pitmans), and South Africa (Chalimbana), all of which have had an influence on the breed in New Zealand.

In 1977 the Dominican Bullmastiff Club NZ was formed, and remains the only Bullmastiff speciality club in New Zealand. Although it is a nationwide club, it caters mainly to the middle to lower parts of North Island. It became a recognized club in 1985, when it held its first ribbon parade. The first open show was held in 1989 and the first championship show on 2 September 1993. Best in Show at the latter was awarded to the home-bred NZ Ch. Oakcroft First Edition, a fawn bitch born on 16 May 1991 (by NZ Ch. Burgowood Anzac Major (Imp. Aust.) out of NZ Ch. Silver Lisa of Mors). On 31 August 1994 Best in Show went to NZ Ch. Boston of Clayburn, a brindle dog born on 24 November 1991 (by NZ Ch. Saxon of Blueflash out of Rangatira Katie) and bred and owned by Mr P. Mitchell. In both 1995 and 1996 Best in Show was again NZ Ch. Oakcroft First Edition; the judge in 1995 was Mr S. Nicholas of Australia while in 1996 it was Mrs K. Cannon of Australia. The Best in Show on 3 September 1997 was awarded to NZ Ch. Vance of Bullmanor; the judge was Mr A. Rostron of the UK. This brindle dog was born on 3 June 1994 (by Alstan Tell Ya Wot out of L-Paw Red Enna), and was bred by Mr G. Lawrence and owned by Mrs L. Storey.

At the Nationals, New Zealand most prestigious show (held annually), Bullmastiff numbers have slowly increased to about twenty-five. Entries at the Bullmastiff Club Speciality Championship Show started with sixty-two entries in 1993 and have decreased grad-

ually since that time. At all-breed championship shows ten is considered a good turn-out, and it is not unusual for there to be only one or
two entries. However, over the last five years the quality of exhibits
has improved greatly, as evidenced by the increase in group and in-
show placings.

The 1990s have seen a continued improvement in the dogs in New
Zealand through the efforts of some dedicated breeders using selec-
tive breeding programmes. Late 1997 saw the first American import,
the red bitch Am./Can. & Int. Ch. Cross's Splash Brandy (by Int. Ch.
Kastles Barb'Eric Obsession out of Int. Ch. Barb'Eric Jim-Dandy
Mandy). She was imported in whelp and produced five puppies on
29 December 1997 by Am./Can. Ch. Willowoods Barb'Eric Mufusa.
This should prove an exciting new bloodline for Mr and Mrs
Lichtwark of Kugel Kennels.

Southern Africa

Bullmastiffs of the Farcroft Kennels of Mr Mosley were imported
from the UK in the mid-1920s by Mrs Heard of South West Africa.
However, between 1928 and 1940 Bullmastiffs were imported in
large numbers by the De Beers Diamond Mining Company for use as
guard dogs at the mines at Kimberley; the De Beers prefix used for
these Bullmastiffs was Adamant. In 1938 the company imported Ch.
Springwell Major (by Ch. Roger of the Fenns out of Lady Dinah of
Springwell), bred by Messrs W. and G. K. Richardson.

Mr O. J. Goddard of Greystokes Kennels, Vereeniging, owned and
bred a large number of Bullmastiffs from 1938, and did a great deal
for the breed in South Africa over the next decade. His dogs included
Adamant Quick March (sired by Ch. Springwell Major), Sup. SA Ch.
Adamant Baker (purchased from Mr Darke of Johannesburg, who
himself bought the dog from De Beers), and SA Ch. Greystokes
Ferdinand of Le Tasyll (by Maritime Fearless out of Penelope of Le
Tasyll), bred by Mrs D. J. Nash of the UK and imported by Mr
Goddard in 1945. Greystokes Ferdinand proved to be a very success-
ful show dog, winning three Best in Shows at all-breeds
championship shows. He was also used extensively at stud, and as
such went on to improve the standard of the South African
Bullmastiffs immensely.

Notable dogs imported into South Africa from the UK at the time
included Battle Grip of Bulmas (bred by Mr C. R. Leeke) and SA Ch.

SA Ch. Tauson Zin Zan of Noshkazan Bullmastiff of the Year SA 1997.

Andy of Buttonoak (bred by Mr and Mrs Terry), both of which were owned by Mr G. Lindsay-Forrester of the Deblyn prefix. Also imported were SA Ch. Maritime Tornado, Ajax of Buttonoak, Ascelin of Buttonoak, Battle Cry of Bulmas, Baroness of Bulmas, Lavender Nina, and Agenta of Buttonoak, all owned by Mr Rix. Bagdannes Bulstaff Jolly Roger and Bulstaff Amaryllis were both imported and owned by Mr G. Behrman.

In the 1950s Mr and Mrs Charles Louw of the Rosy-Morn Kennels did much to improve the quality of the breed. The most notable of their dogs was SA Ch. Bagdannes London Limey of Rosy-Morn, bred by Mr G. Behrman. Others included SA Ch. Bull Bull of Rosy-Morn, SA Ch. Rosy-Morn Sir Gallahad of Bulwark (bred by Mr and Mrs J. S. B. Taylor), SA Ch. Nelly of Rosy-Morn, and SA Ch. Sparlet of Rosy-Morn. The Louws also bred SA Ch. Zombie of Rosy-Morn (owned by Mr C. Erasmus), SA Ch. Valdane's Bachelor Boy of Rosy-Morn (owned by Mr Behrman), SA Ch. Rosy-Morn Bombadier of Bulwark (owned by Mr and Mrs Taylor), and SA Ch. Vanbulls Tessio of Rosy-Morn (owned by Mr and Mrs G. van Staden). Butch of Charmerlyn, sired by Charmerlyns Timmy of Rosy-Morn out of Honey of Dorian Mode, was owned by Mr M. R. Jardine. Today his niece, Mrs Mary Schoeman, together with her husband Piet, is following in her uncle's footsteps, having inherited his love for the breed.

Other breeders and exhibitors during the 1950s were Mr A. T. Darke of Johannesburg, Mr S. W. Fieldgate, breeder of the well-known SA Ch. Lidbury Red Top, his son Mr W. H. Fieldgate (Bloodriver Kennel), Mr and Mrs L. C. Glover (Glovedene), Mr G. Lindsay-Forrest (Deblyn), Mrs C. Vowles (Garryglen), Mrs L. Raubenheimer, Mrs H. Crispin-Street (Crispin), and Mr I. Lax (Diana's).

Although most of the development of the breed at the time took place in the Transvaal, in the Cape Mrs D. R. Montagu of the Blandford Kennels was breeding and showing Bullmastiffs with some success. In 1963 her son, Mr J. Montagu, brought an important import to South Africa from the UK, namely SA Ch. Bulstaff Taurus of Blandford, bred by Mr and Mrs R. Short. Mr C. Swanepoel of the Orange Free State began breeding in the early 1960s. He purchased dogs from Mr Behrman, and from Mr A. Furman he purchased Rover of Steymar, which later went on to become a champion.

SA Ch. Rainel Gilda of Chizlehurst (left), SA Ch. Chizelhurst Chascah (middle), and SA Ch. Chizlehurst Chimurenga.

SA Ch. Groves Bald of Chevael.

In the 1970s James and Liz Turner of the Stillwater prefix became actively involved with Bullmastiffs, breeding and showing extensively. James has judged the breed at open show level, and has held the positions of Chairman of the Bullmastiff Club of Southern Africa and Chairman and President of the Zululand Kennel Club. He has also owned or bred seven champions, the best known of which was SA Ch. Rainel Enrico of Stillwater, who was awarded the title National Bullmastiff in 1989. SA Ch. Stillwater Chancellor, owned and bred by James and Liz, has been Best Bullmastiff Dog of the Year in Natal for 1995 and 1996, while SA Ch. Stillwater Carouse of Eaglehill was Best Bullmastiff Bitch for 1995. James and Liz are still active in the breed today.

The Wellmeadow Kennel was first registered in 1981 by Stewart and Bobby Bain with the purchase of Leblon Angie. She was only ever mated to Jokukids Greg, but out of the second mating she produced three champions, namely SA Ch. Wellmeadows Inkunzie, SA Ch. Wellmeadows Hister, and SA Ch. Wellmeadows Nandi. Hister and Nandi went on to produce several Champions themselves, while Inkunzie also sired several champions. The majority of these dogs were free of hip dysplasia, and great emphasis was placed on the fact that they were bred with sound temperaments, this being considered all important by their breeders. Wellmeadow Bullmastiffs are still being bred today from Indaba of Wellmeadows (sired by Wellmeadows Bonsella of Tauson) and Wellmeadows Thika.

Don and Sue Spooner, although involved with Bullmastiffs for over twenty-seven years, only commenced breeding in 1985 under their Sondu prefix. Their original bitch was Jokukid Cressida of Sondu, from whom all their present stock is descended. They have tended to concentrate on dogs of the brindle colour. Some of their more well-known dogs include SA Ch. Sondu Tristan (born in 1988), SA Ch. Sondu Casca (born 1992, and Top Sire in 1997), SA Ch. Sondu Endore of Lucksdragon, and of course SA Ch. Sondu Imogen of Canonbury (owned by Mrs Sylvia Shorter).

Nicky Robertson's interest in Bullmastiffs began in 1979. She later purchased the bitch Rainels Gilda of Chizlehurst from the Rainel Kennel, who became the foundation bitch of the Chizlehurst Kennel. Rainels Gilda gave birth to four champions, namely SA Ch. Chizlehurst Chimureuga and SA Ch. Chizlehurst Chanda (both sired by Sondu Thabo), and SA Ch. Chizlehurst Chascan and Chizlehurst Charka of Gameguard (both sired by Sondu Casca). Nicky has recently imported from the UK Lombardy Miss Charming of Chizlehurst, bred by Mr and Mrs J. Price.

Robin Coen first became involved with the breed in the mid-1980s with Sunnyfields Nonna, and later acquired the dog Wellmeadow Bonsella of Tauson. In 1992 this dog sired SA Ch. Kimatsu of Tauson, who qualified as a champion in 1994. She was mated to SA Ch. Rainel Enrico of Stillwater, and produced from this litter SA Ch. Tauson Zeetan Torus of Noshkazan and SA Ch. Tauson Zin Zan of Noshkazan. Torus was Bullmastiff of the Year 1996 and Reserve for 1997, while Zin Zan was Bullmastiff of the Year for 1997 and Reserve for 1996. At the time of writing Robin's wife, Nadia, was Secretary of the Bullmastiff Club of Southern Africa, and both she and Robin remain very much involved with the management of the club.

Piet and Mary Schoeman of the Chevael Bullmastiffs also became involved with the breed in the mid-1980s. They later purchased Groves Bald of Chevael, who won his first Challenge Certificate at his first show and went on to gain his title very shortly after this. He was sired by Anubis Ranofer out of Valleyvines Bonny, and is himself the sire of the Supreme Best Puppy for 1997 and Best Male Puppy 1997.

Ronald Folentine of Gamekeeper Bullmastiffs similarly joined the breed in the mid-1980s. Since then he has bred several champions, and today is doing well with SA Ch. Rodja Angel Ambrose of Gamekeeper (by Gamekeeper Elated Emperor out of Gamekeeper Tricky Treveros) and Blazing Bolo of Gamekeeper (sired by Marabrae Hades out of Pedegry Zealous).

After many years as very successful breeders of Mastiffs in the UK, Mr and Mrs Shorter of the Canonbury Bullmastiffs emigrated to South Africa and eventually fell for Bullmastiffs. Their involvement with the breed began in earnest in 1992, since when they have progressed extremely well. Three of their most well-known dogs are SA Ch. Lorand Superbrat of Canonbury (sired by Wellmeadow Umlilo of Fires out of Lorand Storm), who was Best Cape Dog in 1994, 1995, and 1996; SA Ch. Jossarium Primus of Canonbury (sired by Ankaret Hagar out of Kimken Jingle), who went on to win Best Cape Dog in 1997; and SA Ch. Sondu Imogen of Canonbury (sired by SA Ch. Sondu Casca out of Dorcas of Sondu), bred by Don and Sue Spooner, who was Bullmastiff Bitch of the Year in 1996 and 1997.

Steve and Carole King of the Eaglehill Bullmastiffs became associated with the breed in 1993 when they purchased a very well-bred pair in SA Ch. Stillwater Cordite of Eaglehill and SA Ch. Stillwater Carouse of Eaglehill (both sired by SA Ch. Rianel Enrico of Stillwater out of Kimken Magician). Carouse won Best Natal Bitch in 1995.

Steven and Tina Stewart purchased their first Bullmastiff from Nicky Robertson. This was Chizlehurst Charka, who won his first Challenge Certificate at the age of eleven months and went on to gain the title of Champion soon after. The Stewarts have had further successes with Eaglehill Burgundy and Chizlehurst Chamasinga of Gameguard, who was awarded her first Challenge Certificate at the tender age of eight months; by the age of eleven months, she had won three Challenge Certificates and three Best Puppy awards.

Today the breed is gaining interest throughout Southern Africa and should, with the dedication of the breeders named above and many others like them, face a successful and prosperous future.

The Bullmastiff Club of Southern Africa

The foundations of the Bullmastiff Club of Southern Africa were laid when a group of enthusiasts met in Johannesburg in 1954. This group later drafted a constitution, and an application for affiliation to The Kennel Union of Southern Africa (KUSA) was lodged in October of that year; this was accepted and was published in KUSA's gazette in March 1955. Membership in the first year numbered just twenty-nine. The Breed Standard first used was taken from a book of the breed written by Mary Prescot. This was later replaced by The Kennel Club (UK) Breed Standard, supplied by KUSA and adopted in 1973.

Since then the club has grown hugely so that the present-day membership not only includes members from Southern Africa but also from across the world. The club now holds one championship and two non-championship shows annually in the Transvaal, together with a further annual inter-provincial show in northern Natal. Along with these shows there are fun days, breed clinics, and social get-togethers organized by the energetic efforts of the officers and committee.

The way home. Ch. Saturn of Graecia with Alan Rostron.

Useful Addresses

Bullmastiff Clubs

British Bullmastiff League
Secretary: Mr D. Higginson
32 Breverston Road
Tipton
West Midlands

Bullmastiff Association
Secretary: Mrs M. Rostron
Graecia
11 Nicolas Road
Chorlton-cum-Hardy
Manchester
M21 9LG

Northern Bullmastiff Club
Secretary: Mrs D. Massey
37 Low Moor Lane
Woolley
Wakefield
West Yorkshire

Southern Bullmastiff Society
Secretary: Mr B. Blunden
Evesdrop
Epping Road
Nazing
Essex

**Welsh and West of England
Bullmastiff Society**
Secretary: Mr D. Oliff
Wyaston
Woodside
Woolaston
Lydney
Gloucestershire
GL15 6PA

**Bullmastiff Society of
Scotland**
Secretary: Mrs L. Pope
83 Cornalee Gardens
Glasgow
G53 7EB

Bullmastiff Club of Ireland
Secretary: Mr D. Gaffney
119 Ballygall Parade
Fingas
East Dublin
Ireland

Kennel Clubs

American Kennel Club Inc.
51 Madison Avenue
New York
NY10010
USA

Australian National Kennel Council
PO Box 285
Red Hill South
Victoria 3937
Australia

Fédération Cynologique Internationale
12 rue Leopold II
B-6530 Thuin
Belgium

Irish Kennel Club
Fotterell House
Greenmount Office Park
Dublin 6
Ireland

The Kennel Club (UK)
1–5 Clarges Street
Piccadilly
London
W1Y 8AB
UK

Kennel Union of Southern Africa
PO Box 2659
Cape Town 8000
South Africa

New Zealand Kennel Club Inc.
Prosser Street
Elsdon
Private Bag 50903
Porirua
Wellington
New Zealand

Bibliography

American Kennel Club, *Judge's Application Process Handbook* (1997).

American Kennel Club, *Rules Applying to Dog Shows* (1996).

Australian National Kennel Council, *Judge's Training Programme* (1997).

Billinghurst, Dr Ian, *Give Your Dog a Bone* (1993).

Buffon, Comte de Georges Louis Leclere, *Histoire Naturelle,* 36 vols [1746–89], trans. W. Smellie, *Natural History*: from Parson, Daniel (ed.), *In Praise of Dogs*, Country Life Books (1936); trans, Gmelin, *Natural History*: from Ash, Edward, *Dogs: Their History and Development*, Ernest Benn (1927).

Caius, Dr Johannes, *De Canibus Britannicis* [1570], trans. Abraham Fleming, *Of English Dogges* [1576], Denlinger (1947).

Canadian Kennel Club, *Dog Show Rules and Regulations* (1997).

Craven, Arthur C., *The Bull-Mastiff as I Know It* (1932).

Dagleish, E. F., *The Dog Breeder's Manual* (1951).

Edward, Duke of York, *The Master of Game* [1406–13], W., A. and F. Ballie-Grohman (1904).

Evans, J. M. and White, K., *The Book of the Bitch* Henston (1988).

Fleming, Abraham (trans.), *Of English Dogges* [1576], *see* Caius.

Frankling, Eleanor, *Practical Dog Breeding and Genetics*, Stanley Paul (1998).

Gordon, John F., *The Staffordshire Bull Terrier*, Popular Dogs (1986).

Harmar, H., *Dogs and How to Breed Them*, (1979).

Hedberg, Karen, *The Dog Owner's Manual* (1989).

Hubbard, Clifford B., *The Bullmastiff*, Nimrod Press (1957) reprinted 1988.

Jesse, George, R., *Anecdotes of Dogs* (1846)

Kennel Club Stud Book, The Kennel Club (annually).

Kennel Union of Southern Africa, *Aspirant Breed Judge's Qualifying Scheme* (1998).

Lanting, Fred L., *Canine Hip Dysplasia* (1981).

Lawrence, John, *The Sportsman's Repositary* (1820).

Manwood, John, *A Treatist of the Lawes of the Forest* [1615]: from Hubbard, Clifford, B., *The Bullmastiff, see* Hubbard.

Oliff, D.B., *The Mastiff and Bullmastiff,* Boydell Press (1989).

Page-Elliot, Rachel, *Dog Steps*, Howell Book House Inc.

Smythe, R. H., *The Breeding and Rearing of Dogs* (1979).

Smythe, R. H., *The Dog: Structure and Movement*, W. Foulsham & Co. Ltd (1948).

Spira, Harold R., *Canine Terminology*, Harper & Row (1982).

Willis, Malcolm B., *Practical Genetics for Dog Breeders*, Witherby (1992).

Index